Rebuilding
the Walls

Rebuilding the Walls

A Challenge to the Church from Ezra and Nehemiah

Stuart Bell

Sovereign World

Sovereign World Ltd
PO Box 777
Tonbridge
Kent TN11 0ZS
England

ISBN 1 85240 368 3

Cover design by CCD, www.ccdgroup.co.uk
Typeset by CRB Associates, Reepham, Norfolk
Printed by Clays Ltd, St Ives plc

Dedication

I dedicate this book to Irene, my wife and best friend, and to my children, Andrew, Becki and her husband Glen, and David. I am proud of them all.

Contents

Acknowledgements

A big thank you to those who have helped me with this project.

A special thank you to Val Seager, my trusted typist and PA, and to Rita Blackler for her many hours of proofreading.

Thank you to Pete and Hannah Atkins, Godfrey Birtill, Chris Bowater, Trish Morgan and Francois van Niekerk for their contributions and perspectives.

To Tim Pettingale, who, like Cyrus, opened a door for me with Sovereign World.

Finally, to New Life Christian Fellowship, Lincoln and the Ground Level Team – the best people in the world to serve.

Foreword

Stuart has the gift of 'connecting'. In a most relaxing way he seems to bring the most diverse people together in profitable connections. I have had the privilege of seeing him do this and I don't even think he knows when it happens.

This same gift seems to work in his writing. In this book he connects people, historic events and his personal experiences to form an amazing tapestry in which the Scripture and God's plan remains central.

As you read, I believe this anointing and gift will connect you with God's power and with God's plan. It will cause a holy connection between you and your role to help build a 'strong and effective church taking central position in society.'

I dream, with Stuart, of such a powerful church and also share the conviction that this book will contribute to it becoming a growing reality.

Through his friendly style and unique humour Stuart succeeds in challenging us all to stay in step with God's restoration process. However, it goes deeper than that. From his rich insight I have personally gained practical gems of truth that have equipped me further and left a fresh hope in my heart that God will complete the work He started!

I'm sure it will do the same for you and much more!

Francois van Niekerk
Senior Pastor of Hatfield Christian Church
Pretoria, South Africa

Introduction

Ezra and Nehemiah record the return of the Jewish exiles from Babylonia and the rebuilding of the Temple and walls of Jerusalem. These books have fascinated me for a number of years as they record great changes in the spiritual climate of the day. After years of captivity, things begin to move quickly. Days of disappointment turn into days of destiny. 'The book of Ezra reveals the providential intervention of the God of heaven on behalf of his people.'[1]

These are challenging books that hold great relevance for today. I believe that in Britain, we are seeing in some measure a rebuilding take place. It is my desire to see this rebuilding in church life continue so that our cities, towns and villages may be transformed and changed.

2 Chronicles 36 reveals the sorry story of the fall of Jerusalem. God's people had resisted His ways and had mocked His messengers. The Babylonians captured Jerusalem and a great slaughter took place under Nebuchadnezzar. A remnant was then carried off to Babylon to serve the king's purposes and the heart was ripped out of God's special city, Jerusalem.

> 'They set fire to God's temple and broke down the wall of Jerusalem; they burned all the palaces and destroyed everything of value there.' (2 Chronicles 36:19)

After a dormant period of seventy years, which had been prophesied by Jeremiah, a new era was about to begin.

> 'In the first year of Cyrus king of Persia, in order to fulfil the word of the LORD spoken by Jeremiah . . .' (Ezra 1:1)

11

Notice it was the first year of the new reign. It is my belief that prophetic words hang over our nation and that greater days are ahead for the Church of Jesus.

Three key things were rebuilt in the days of Ezra and Nehemiah. These give a useful picture of a shift that needs to take place if we are to see this new day open up for the Church in Britain. Firstly, the **altar** was rebuilt. It was essential that, after years of captivity, this central dimension of worship should be unlocked. Ezra 3 outlines the need for sacrifices to be made again. The rebuilt altar symbolised the importance of personal devotion and cleansing. The sacrifice prescribed by the Law of Moses had to return and the heart of the city was to be personal worship of the Living God. It was this that marked God's people out and made them different from the nations around them.

Secondly, the rebuilding of the **temple** followed on quickly. This was not just a call to personal devotion, but also a call to corporate community, and for a people who are joined by purpose and destiny.

Thirdly, the **walls** had to be established again. The city was viewed as cursed until strong walls protected its people. The whole city needed to be affected and changed. This book seeks to follow the story of rebuilding which moved on to the transforming of a whole city.

This Old Testament story teaches us what God can do even in days of exile, and that city walls can be rebuilt in fifty-two days (see Nehemiah 6:15), if it's God's hand that oversees the rebuilding. In fact, it is very clear that the favour of the Lord is extended in a special way during this period of time. On the first day of a new month Ezra safely arrived in Jerusalem, *'for the gracious hand of his God was on him'* (Ezra 7:9). And Ezra also said,

> *'Because the hand of the* Lord *my God was on me, I took courage and gathered leading men from Israel to go up with me.'*
> (Ezra 7:28)

Other references to God's hand are found in Ezra 8:18, 22 and 31 and Nehemiah 2:8. God's favour was being extended. He was keeping His people safe and secure, and they were marked out for success.

Over a number of years a new song has been emerging over the British churches. A refreshing wind has been blowing and the strains of 'This is the year of the favour of the Lord' are being heard. Graham Cooke and other prophetic voices have in fact designated this very year as the year of the Lord's favour. (Graham Cooke is a recognised prophet associated with Tony Morton in Southampton, England.) Things change when the gracious hand of the Lord is upon us.

As the people began to return to Jerusalem a prophetic voice began to be heard again. This was the voice that brought strength and conviction to the builders.

> *'The hands of Zerubbabel have laid the foundation of this temple; his hands will also complete it.'*   (Zechariah 4:9)

Zechariah the prophet, sensing the new day had arrived, declared that no opposition or obstacle would stop God's work. This was going to be a work of the Spirit,

> *'This is the word of the* Lord *to Zerubbabel: "Not by might nor by power, but by my Spirit," says the* Lord *Almighty.'*
> (Zechariah 4:6)

For transformation to take place we will need to experience God's hand and God's Spirit in our land.

Note
1.   *NIV Bible Commentary* (Hodder & Stoughton) p. 682.

PART 1

Rebuilding

Chapter 1

Rebuilding – the Altar

I had always wanted to visit 'The Church on the Way' in Los Angeles and when an invitation came to attend the annual Pastors' Conference, I immediately pencilled-in the dates in my diary. An early morning American Airlines flight from Pittsburgh flew me over the sprawling city and as we landed, I was filled with excitement at the possibility of seeing a number of places I had never dreamed I would visit. In the business of travel, it had been a long time since I had been filled with such a feeling of child-like anticipation. The conference lived up to my expectations and I also had the joy of meeting Jean Darnell, who I had not seen for many years. I recalled how important she had been in the encouragement she had given to me in my early years of ministry. This trip was going to have a lot to do with roots and foundations, not only in my personal life, but also in helping me to gain a greater understanding of the roots of the church movement that I am thrilled to be a part of today. Joseph Garlington, from Pittsburgh, had kindly invited me to accompany him to Los Angeles and on a free afternoon, he asked me what I would like to see. I immediately spoke of Azusa Street, Bonny Bray Street and Angelus Temple.

He replied, 'We can do most of that but you must also visit The Dream Centre.'

Our first port-of-call was a little house on Bonny Bray Street where William J. Seymour, an Afro-American, had lived. Outside this small house in the early 1900s Seymour had preached to large crowds and had then began to minister in a reclaimed warehouse and horse stable at 312 Azusa Street. From this small location, the world was to be impacted by the Pentecostal movement.

We then visited the impressive Angelus Temple, which was established by Amy Semple-McPherson (1890–1944). It was this lady who founded the Foursquare Movement of which Church on the Way is now a part. I avidly took photographs, not only of the building, but also of the glass cabinets that were filled with crutches, wheelchairs, plaster casts and discarded medical apparatus – all testimonies of God's healing power through her ministry. The buildings were undergoing a renovation programme to bring them back to their former glory. This was for me a visual sign of spiritual renovations that were also taking place. We had not realised before our visit that Angelus Temple was now being brought into the vision of 'The Dream Centre', the very place that Joseph had insisted we visit. An old hospital on the edge of Hollywood displayed a large red sign that could be seen for miles around with the words, 'THE DREAM CENTRE'.

The activity and life I encountered for the next few hours challenged me deeply as I witnessed dynamic Christianity in action. Over one hundred Christian ministries were housed within the complex and at the hub was Matthew Barnett (who looks annoyingly young and vibrant) leading a living church. This vision has impacted many people with the good news of Jesus, involving ministry to addicts, prostitutes, gang members and AIDS sufferers. The evening meeting was one of the best I have been in as the love of Jesus oozed among us. It was also a great surprise to meet my good friend Paul Scanlon, who was the guest speaker. As we made our way back on the crowded freeway, I was deeply grateful to God. Not only had I touched something of the roots of the Pentecostal movement, but I had also witnessed a re-building that in the days ahead may bring even greater fruit for the Kingdom of God.

That night I slept heavily and contentedly. In the morning I decided to walk from my hotel to the conference – not a good idea! Crossing roads in Lincoln, England is rather different from a stroll in Van Nuys. By a miracle of grace I eventually arrived, but not before I had seen another important landmark. My morning saunter caused me to pass St Andrew's Episcopalian church where Dennis Bennett had been impacted by a fresh move of the Holy Spirit in the 1960s. I immediately kicked into 'nostalgia mode' as I contemplated how his book *Nine O'clock in the Morning*[1] had brought new hope to believers in Britain, and contributed to the heralding-in of the Charismatic movement in our nation. This brief visit to Los Angeles reminded me of my roots. I had been shaped years earlier by my involvement with the Pentecostals and it had been a Pentecostal who had laid hands on me for the Baptism in the Holy Spirit. I had immediately been thrust into what we now speak of as the Charismatic movement.

On my return home I began to piece my experiences together and was reminded of another day away that had affected my thinking. Bill and Melinda Fish, from Pittsburgh, USA, were visiting our church. I decided we would 'do the tourist thing' and had already inflicted on them a whirlwind trip around Lincoln and had then driven them to Epworth, the home of the Wesleys. As Americans I'm sure that the Fish's were expecting to find 'Wesley-burgers' being sold on the streets of the town. However, any evidence of former glory days had to be searched for. It was almost as though this sleepy community had little knowledge of the importance of what had happened centuries earlier and, having been brought up in the Methodist Church I had witnessed its decline. I had often travelled around the Methodist circuit when I was boy, listening to my dad preach. My impressions were of small groups of ageing, but sincere people fighting for survival. I stood on Samuel Wesley's grave, the place where John Wesley chose to preach from because of his exclusion from the Anglican Church building. However, just a few friends and an assortment of birds, rather than crowds eager to hear the gospel, surrounded me. I have a photograph to prove the authenticity of my story, and my prayer is that God will move again by His Holy Spirit within the Methodist Church.

So what have these stories got to do with the re-building of the altar in the days of Ezra? Simply this: the people of God had been in exile and Jerusalem was in a place of devastation; the city of God, which had meant to be a blessing to the nations, lay in ruins. Stories of God's blessing were locked away in the past and it was time for men and women of faith to believe God once again. The days of Ezra and Nehemiah became days of re-building. As we shall see later, God began to raise up significant leaders with vision who could challenge the people of the day. They had no need to settle for the status quo but could begin to make a difference. The starting place in the programme of restoration was the re-building of the altar. The altar is the place where individuals can have their sins forgiven and where they become realigned to the will of God. The early Pentecostals began to rebuild an altar. Personal worship of the Living God began to be important again. This heart in earlier years had been carried by John Wesley, known by some as the father of Pentecostalism.[2]

There are always seasons of rebuilding in churches and it is my belief that in Britain we have seen, over the last thirty years or so, a growing emphasis of the importance of the re-building of an altar. This has been marked wonderfully by a new surge of worship, which has changed the shape of church life in our nation. Just as Charles Wesley, the 'sweet singer' of Methodism,[3] captured this re-building in his many hymns, so we too have seen the emergence of our very own 'sweet singers' who have influenced the church of today. Graham Kendrick was one of the forerunners of the new sound of worship ascending from the British church. This has become a 'make way' call and we are enjoying the blessing of it.

> *'Then Jeshua son of Jozadak and his fellow priests and Zerubbabel son of Shealtiel and his associates began to build the altar of the God of Israel to sacrifice burnt offerings on it, in accordance with what is written in the Law of Moses the man of God.'* (Ezra 3:2)

It took many people to rebuild the altar and Jeshua and Zerubbabel began to face the challenge. After years of mediocrity in our own nation, God saw to it that altars would be restored. In the 1960s and 1970s the baptism in the Holy Spirit began to move beyond the Pentecostal churches. In England, on September 29th, 1964, Michael Harper formed the influential Fountain Trust, which soon published the *Renewal* magazine. The Charismatic movement spread across all boundaries and the Roman Catholic Church was impacted by a move at Duquesne University in Pittsburgh, USA. South African Assemblies of God minister, David Du Plessis, affectionately known as 'Mr Pentecost', said that God had told him to go to the Roman Catholics and that thousands were receiving the Holy Spirit. A new movement was emerging. One stream of this movement began to focus, not only upon the renewal of the church, but also upon seeing the church experience restoration. The group originally known as the House Church movement began to look for a church that carried qualities of New Testament life. It is of great interest to me that teams began to come to the fore with a heart to see churches strengthened and restored. There was also an emergence of church-planting strategies. Within new teams it seemed as though God gave each a 'sweet singer'. Graham Kendrick linked with Roger Forster and the Ichthus group of churches, Dave Fellingham linked with Terry Virgo and the New Frontiers network, David Hadden joined with Bryn Jones and Covenant Ministries International, and Noel Richards joined with Gerald Coates and the Pioneer team, to name a few. In our own setting God linked us with Chris Bowater who, through the years, has found his ministry moving out from the local church in Lincoln to the nations of the world. In fact, Lincoln New Life has been blessed with a number of talented songwriters who are seeking to express the life of God among us. This has been a personal joy to me as we seek to make our small contribution in the rebuilding within our nation. I have invited Chris Bowater and Trish Morgan (who was part of the band Heartbeat, and is now a songwriter and worship leader among us) to share their own perspectives of the changes that they have witnessed with regard to worship in the British churches. However, before they share, perhaps I could recount some of the struggles experienced in the rebuilding of an altar to the Lord.

The journey into the new styles of worship was painful for some. Newly found liberty, on occasions, also seemed to bring the strangest people to the forefront who would not be averse to offering to 'lengthen people's legs' after the meeting. It was in one of these charismatic gatherings where I well remember this thought-provoking prophecy: 'Thus saith the Lord, it is thus. "Thus saith the Lord it is thus. Thus saith the Lord, it is not thus, it is thus." ' The prophecy was followed by the customary intake of breath, 'Hmm', as people sought to respond appropriately to the word. I decided it was a little too deep for me, and among the rattle of tambourines and charismatic two-step its significance seemed to fade. Every meeting seemed to include 'look at the person next to you, and say' and conclude with 'I love you with the love of the Lord', or 'Bind us Together'. I remember my own self-consciousness as I moved from the hands together and eyes closed position to hands half-raised with palms lifted heavenward. I later discovered that this was the charismatic way and that the fully extended arms version was the property of the Pentecostals.

Others struggled as pressure descended, not always from

heaven, to discover the joys of dance. Again the
two versions. The charismatic choreographed cɪ
the more wholehearted leaping. I must confess I
the leaping variety and left the other kind for the ɪ
Even clapping to the songs caused major problems fᴏ   , and
we did seem to have nights that were both 'happy aᵢd clappy'.
However, there were some interesting things happening on the
periphery of meetings where we witnessed the 'struggle pains' of
many who were pushing though into a genuine and personal
encounter of worship. Altars were being rebuilt and traditions
were being challenged.

Worship and praise and the crossroads – *Chris Bowater*

I guess that this title at least suggests that it is still on a journey.
Where the Church is at, in respect to praise and worship, and
where it is heading, is in some ways determined by its history.
The theological territory has perhaps never been in dispute. The
contemporary stylistic debate has largely become embraced,
though at times admittedly, only tolerated. There are, however,
new theological and cultural challenges facing the 21st century
worshipping Church. So, what is the story that has brought us to
a time and place where once again everything is up for review?

Each generation has faced the challenge of embracing the
new, finding themselves often in conflict to traditional thought
and practice. As far back as Pope Gregory, The Roman Catholic
Church tried to canonize music. There are still orders of the
Church whole-heartedly subscribing to the Gregorian chant. As
beautiful an art form as it is, and as well established as it became,
time has passed and the mainstream of the Catholic Church has
left it behind. History reveals many attempts to canonize music.
The 'we have found it' movements in time became mere monu-
ments – sad and fossilized relics of a people unable or unwilling
to adopt and reflect change. Calvin and Luther were locked into
a theological and creative battle. Calvin insisted that only God's
Word was worthy to be sung in God's praise; hymns and human
composition were forbidden. Luther borrowed tunes from the
secular arena in his day and for that, received much criticism.
Priests of the mid-eighteenth century generally rejected art
music and generally set out to create a more pure 'church music'.
The Salvation Army was vilified for their militant rhythms that

lacked solemnity. Sankey and Moody shocked with their use of the waltz, made famous by the composer Johann Strauss, and so it goes on.

More than twenty-five years ago the signs of metamorphosis in worship and praise music in the UK were evident. It was a transformation with far-reaching results. The songs birthed in this nation since that time have touched the nations of the earth and modelled creative, theological and prophetic ways forward. *Scripture in Song* came out of New Zealand. The simplicity and freshness of folk-inspired settings of Bible verses also swept through the nations.

The *Come Together* musical by Jimmy and Carol Owens, and subsequent titles, *If My People* and *The Witness*, introduced many to new styles of worship. These challenged the widely used 'hymn/prayer sandwich'. New publications such as *Youth Praise* and *Songs of Fellowship*, *Mission Praise* and the innovation of *Spring Harvest* (an interdenominational event attracting many thousands over the past two decades) nurtured and released an abundance of new songs into the life of the Church. This middle of the road soft-rock style spawned the emergence of worship teams and the introduction of drums, bass, guitars and keyboards, threatening the long established reign of the piano and organ. More importantly, the long rule of the sole pianist and organist was being challenged. Largely, the prevailing themes were the Father's heart, love for Jesus, and a celebration of joy.

Graham Kendrick emerged as the most significant, cross-denominational writer. His songs had accessible melodies and guitar chords, and were rich with strong theological content, finding acceptance outside of the confines of charismatic renewal.

The growth of new Church, renewal in the established denominations and the emergence of a re-envisioned youth culture in the Pentecostal Church gave rise to worship and praise that was contemporary in style with a new sense of Spirit-led freedom. The Dales Bible Weeks, hosted by Harvest Time Churches and its restoration theology brought a renewed vision of the Church and the Kingdom. An emphasis on the Holy Spirit and, later, the influence of Vineyard Churches, brought a new dimension of devotion, awe and an emphasis on holiness.

These were extraordinary times in the life of the UK Church. For me to be involved alongside Graham Kendrick, Noel Richards,

Dave Bilborough and Dave Fellingham shaping a new worship culture in the 1980s and early 1990s, was an awesome honour. The ministries of each of us writing and leading praise and worship grew out of networks of strong relationships. It is impossible to disregard the significance of these networks and the key friendships with apostolic leaders. It is also significant that these relationships are still in place today; Graham with Ichthus and Roger Forster, Noel with Pioneer and Gerald Coates, Dave Fellingham with New Frontiers and Terry Virgo, and Dave Bilborough with John Noble, Team Spirit. There is also, Pioneer and myself in association with AoG and Ground Level, whilst in a committed friendship with John Shelbourne and Stuart Bell.

In the mid to later part of the 1990s worship and praise was impacted by the sounds and styles of Integrity Music from the USA and Hillsong from Australia. However, there has been an accelerated growth of young British writers led by Martin Smith of Delirious fame, Matt Redman and Stuart Townsend. Again, these ministries have been nurtured in and grown out of strong apostolic and network relationships. The key thought of this generation is summed up in Matt Redman's song, 'When the Music Fades'. He wrote, 'I'm coming back to the heart of worship, it's all about You, Jesus'.

This brings us to a place that I have called 'Worship and Praise at the Cross Roads'.

There are many challenges, changes and questions to be faced by this 21st century Church:

- In order to be truly rooted in a Christian culture, today's songs need to re-state the values and foundations of the Faith. Expect to see a re-emphasis on the Cross, Salvation, Forgiveness, Hope, the Resurrection, the Second Coming and Heaven.

- Theological objectivity needs to balance the pre-occupation with subjective feelings and a mere emotional response.

- We should anticipate an increase of co-writing and team worship leading, combating independence and individualism.

- There will be a greater 'mixing up' of traditions and styles as theological streams and musical styles discover and fuse with one another. Freedom and orthodoxy will increasingly be comfortable with each other.

- There will be a growing reaction to a Christian Worship industry that insists on manufacturing the worship agenda rather than reflecting what God is doing at grass roots in the Church.

- Spiritual sons and daughters will rediscover their spiritual parents. Even though the trend to embrace and release youth culture will increase it will be accomplished in the context of prayerful and skilful mentoring.

- The worshipping Church will become more multi-media conscious and worship will be truly more creative and glorious.

- True worship will avoid a 'spectator and audience' mentality. The excellence of performance will become secondary to an excellence of spirit. Character will take pre-eminence above charisma.

- Attitude will be more important than ability.

- The worshipping Church will become increasingly outward looking. The **intimacy** of worship will produce the **engagement** of the Church in local community, national and international care and welfare.

- Brokenness and joy will be the hallmark of this 21st century worshipping Church. Brokenness produces total dependency on God, which, in turn, produces total satisfaction and joy in Him.

There is a re-building and repairing process at work in the Church today. I believe that the vision and desire for worship is being renewed. The journey so far has not been without hazards and mistakes, but it has also been very fruitful. The foundations are good. Now, let a new generation with a desire to complete what has been started step up and walk and live the vision to its fulfilment.

The worship revolution – *Trish Morgan*

The worship revolution started modestly in the late 1960s. If you ever had the opportunity to visit Chard, a small West Country town in Somerset, you would have witnessed one of the centres where the revolution was beginning. As a child I sat in wonder at the joyful and exuberant praise that often consisted of simple four-line songs.

'This Joy, His Joy, overflows,
This Joy, His Joy grows and grows,
This Joy, His joy sets my spirit free,
Thank-you Lord for giving it to me!'

The tunes weren't technical and the rhythm was probably 4/4, but they sang loudly, joyfully, and they sang it through more than twice!

I had been brought up in a Baptist church and when we visited this lively church I witnessed hilarious praise, dancing and clapping. Everyone had a tambourine and it was noisy! Besides that, the pastor's wife regularly banged the swing-doors at the back, which had a formative percussion sound. This along with an organ, piano and squeezebox was all one could call a worship team, not that they probably knew what they were! We didn't have any hymnbooks, only our Bibles. The meetings would go on for hours. It seemed that God had a lot to say via tongues and interpretation, prophetic words, exhortations and ministry of the Word. This was also the first time I became aware of the Holy Spirit.

A time that I will never forget was watching a man with tears rolling down his cheeks dancing even after the music had finished; he just kept on going. People would weep whilst singing that they loved Jesus. I couldn't help but be drawn to this kind of worship, and it was powerful.

A few years later I sat in a school hall as a New Zealand couple called Dale and Dave Garratt began to use Scripture in song. Again these songs were refreshing and liberating. It was the 1970s and our services were shaking off the old 'hymn/prayer' format. It was a freedom that many of us were so thankful for. Musically, the songs we were now singing were beginning to have more form to them beyond a few lines. Often congregations had no songbooks so good memories were required. Visiting speakers would introduce and carry songs from city to city and new songs were taught at united church gatherings.

Another significant milestone was the musical by Jimmy and Carol Owens *Come Together*. It was contemporary in sound and made a profound impact on me as a teenager. The opening bars of the musical were a band sound and began to announce a new contemporary music culture in Christian circles. Soon bands were springing up to play this musical locally and from there quite a few churches inherited what we would know as, 'a worship team'.

As a musician, my 'role' as worship leader came out of a necessity to have someone able to improvise and play by ear. There still wasn't much written music available, but in those early years I learnt a lot about the term 'anointing'.

Cue the 1980s
As the whole renewal movement took shape and embraced the revelation of the Holy Spirit's role in our lives and worship, so the challenge came to have some form of order to our meeting together.

I had been in a fellowship that had practised 'everyone hath!' and we were very body-ministry orientated. Anybody could start a song and, as the keyboard player, I often found myself in 'name that tune and find the right key!' This format did work when you had a small congregation but as they grew in number this became increasingly difficult to manage. It was at this point that we saw a defining of worship styles. Some churches felt comfortable with appointing a 'worship leader'. Their role was either to choose the songs and link them together, or to play alongside a church leader who would do the directional bit and leave the worship leader to play and sing. A lot of our worship expressions began to be heavily influenced by apostolic teaching; hats on, hats off, drums in, drums out, songs of the Kingdom, songs of grace and freedom, restoration, revival. Clearly the teaching of the renewal movement was shaping our hymnology.

By the late 1980s we had a worship explosion on our hands from conferences and worship albums to praise parties; we were in real danger of worshipping worship and our overhead projectors and not God Himself. With the beauty of hindsight, it probably means we were experiencing growing pains, and these new churches are now approximately a quarter of a century old!

Now there is beginning to emerge a more balanced maturing church. Hymns have been rescued and included once again, and in the 1990s younger songwriters brought us a more humble and honest, but also biblical approach, whilst striving for musical excellence. The rediscovery of worship in the 1990s also led certain sections of the church to retrace their spiritual roots. Celtic influences were explored, and even now are incorporated into our worship. Some went on a journey almost despising 'charismatic' worship and the raising of hands routine. Some others simply lost their focus and truly didn't know where they belonged. Others have felt more at home back in a high-church setting. At times we could be guilty of froth and bubble with little connection to the real world, and there is much we could incorporate to counteract this. The involving of other art forms, besides music, is one of the ways we are learning to explore. The worship revolution seems to be in need of another breath.

So, some questions go beyond even the worship issue. Have we lost our passion? No, I don't think so. Are we still joyful! Yes, but we could do with more hilarious, holy chaos. Are we too professional? Only if we don't keep a heart for worship in tension to being musically skilful like the psalmist of old. It's a fine line that needs to be evaluated regularly.

How important is lifestyle and holiness? Do we have a congregation that know the Word of God and long to treasure it? And lastly, and more importantly, do we please God's heart? A responsibility I feel acutely; after all, worship is for Him, first and foremost.

Notes

1. Dennis Bennett, *Nine O'clock in the Morning* (Bridge-Logos Publishers, 1970).
2. James Dunn, *The History of Christianity* (Lion, 1977), p. 618.
3. Skevington-Wood, *The History of Christianity* (Lion, 1977), p. 447.

Chapter 2

Rebuilding – the Temple

The Book of Ezra begins with the enthusiastic family heads of Judah and Benjamin, together with priests and Levites, having prepared to return to Jerusalem to see its temple rebuilt. Friends and neighbours supported them in their travels by giving them valuable articles and livestock. They also had a freewill offering towards their journey. Lists of exiles were made and a variety of people who could trace their family lines headed towards Jerusalem. The city, which had lain in ruins, was to be rebuilt. Commitment levels began to rise as the foundations of the temple were laid. The people were becoming purpose-driven again after years of lethargy. The foundation-laying ceremony produced mixed reactions. People gladly offered to their God, priests put on their vestments, and the instruments of David were brought out of storage. However, many of the older priests and Levites wept aloud. They had memories of more grand structures in times past. There was a strange mingling of exuberant joy and loud weeping:

> *'No-one could distinguish the sound of the shouts of joy from the sound of weeping, because the people made so much noise.'*
>
> (Ezra 3:13)

There was no denying it; a miracle of rebuilding was taking place. There were to be days ahead of pressure and opposition, and on occasion the sounds of building work would be silenced. But stone by stone the temple was being restored. News eventually broke on the third day of the month Adar that *'the temple was completed'* (Ezra 6:15). The altar had been rebuilt and now the temple stood shining in the golden city. If the rebuilt altar points us to the restoring of personal worship to the people of God, then the rebuilt temple speaks of the restoring of corporate worship to His people, the Church.

There is no doubt in my mind that the last thirty years have seen a rebuilding programme taking place in terms of the Church. Traditional church structures have been tested, and new forms of church have begun to emerge. My own experience initially brought me into conflicts that I never looked for. These were often to do with my own naivety and lack of communication skills. There was no doubt that I became impatient with existing churches and longed to see things change. This was also mixed with youthful bravado and the knowledge that my father and grandfather had both found themselves somewhat ostracised from certain church structures due to their desire to follow the way of the Spirit.

In my late teens I was part of a four-piece band called 'The Advocates'. We were associate evangelists with British Youth for Christ and began to travel the length and breadth of the country sharing our faith. We visited schools, colleges, prisons and churches and flourished in the coffee-bar evangelism that sprang up as churches wanted to reach out to the new generation. We rigidly kept our commitment to our local Methodist church and, even though we often returned from our travels in the early hours of Sunday morning, we all made sure we would be in church for the worship service. We were used to the services, though an hour's 'divine worship' did seem a long time. I often wondered why the clock was placed behind the preacher's head if we were meant to remain suitably encouraged. Our church was filled with good people and at the midweek service the more keener were allowed a little more freedom. As part of the Methodist year of evangelism we were invited to take a mission in Lincoln. This involved visiting schools in the city for a week and then holding concerts in our own church building. During this mission over thirty young people became Christians. It seemed obvious that we would invite these new believers to join us at church the following Sunday morning. To our surprise a number came, but after the hour, and long glances at the clock behind the preacher's head, our newfound friends found their first trip to church, shall we say, a little difficult. We speedily met with our minister, briefly outlined our problem and gained permission to meet with the group on Monday evenings in the minister's vestry for 'discipleship', as it is called in the trade. The following Monday arrived but the dingy lighting and the smell of gas was not conducive to spiritual growth. The inevitable happened and, with the full permission of our understanding minister, Friday nights became the gathering time, and our house, the venue. I can honestly say that 'church planting' was not on our agenda, but as time passed it became obvious that we had planted a church by accident. To our joy a few years later, the Methodist church in our area recognised us and offered us their blessing. For a while, however, the relationships were quite strained. The format of the evenings together was simple. Worship songs were sung, usually with the aid of three chords on a solitary guitar, and we studied the Bible together. The next seven years saw the emergence of church that we had not experienced before. Our small world was being transformed as we saw God changing people's lives before our eyes. Our fragile group began to share their faith, and to our amazement more people came to find Christ. We had begun an exciting journey together. Our house seemed to have young people passing through it most of the time, day and night, and eventually we knocked down a wall to accommodate more. Before very long we hired a small hall in the north of the city and fervently tried to discover what we called 'New Testament Christianity'. In our joint quest I was impressed with the church at Antioch. I started to see a church that was not holding on until the return of Jesus, but a vibrant, living community of people with a passion for God and a heart for mission. In the years ahead we were to discover some of the following things that were so evident in Antioch city as described in Acts of the Apostles.

The Antioch church model

Antioch in New Testament days was the influential capital of the Roman province of Syria. The church that emerged there became the birthplace of Christian foreign missions. Its growth and creative structures have remained a challenge to the Church of Jesus through the following centuries.

A church with an evangelical message
The church at Antioch was not birthed following a church-growth seminar, but it appears that its planting came in a very

natural way. Acts 11 tells us that believers had been scattered
through persecution in Jerusalem, and among them were men
from Cyprus and Cyrene who reached as far as Antioch. This was
the first time that the message reached beyond the Jews into the
Gentile world. However, their strategy was simple and had to do
with *'telling them the good news about the Lord Jesus'* (Acts 11:20).
The planting began with a Jesus-centred message and immediately brought results. It was this Jesus message that caused people
to nickname them, 'Christians': *'The disciples were called Christians first at Antioch'* (Acts 11:26).

In Britain in the early 1970s, there were definite signs of Jesus-
centred Christianity returning. In June 1971, in *Time* magazine,
they ran a twelve-page cover story entitled, 'The Jesus Generation'. In various parts of the world a generation desiring to break
out of established church structures was looking to return to
biblical roots.

A church living in evident favour and grace

'The Lord's hand was with them' (Acts 11:21). Barnabas, the
'Mr Grace' of the Jerusalem church, was sent to Antioch to check
out the authenticity of reports of people finding Christ. On
arrival, he detected that all was well.

> *'When he arrived and saw the evidence of the grace of God, he
> was glad and encouraged them all to remain true to the Lord with
> all their hearts.'*   (Acts 11:23)

There was nothing special about these people; they were
simply receiving undeserved favour as the smile of God was upon
them. In fact, this newfound grace was quickly attacked as a
group, demanding that the new believers should be circumcised,
arrived on the scene. This legalistic attack even brought Paul and
Barnabas into a sharp dispute. A council at Jerusalem was called
to bring a ruling, and the grace issue was protected. At the roots
the council decided not to give-in to the pressure of the Judaisers:

> *'No! We believe it is through the grace of our Lord Jesus that we
> are saved, just as they are.'*   (Acts 15:11)

A letter was sent to Antioch affirming that the new 'Christians'
were no longer under the Law and were free to trust in Jesus'

work alone. In the rebuilding of church life, it seems to me that the grace factor is essential. Legalism is to be fought at all cost. What a liberating message the grace message is. This is starkly illustrated in the words of Philip Yancey in his book, *What's So Amazing About Grace*. He writes, 'There is nothing I can do to make God love me more, there is nothing I can do to make God love me less.'[1]

A church carrying effective ministries

In my early life as a Christian I had observed the one-man ministry model and wondered what it would take to see all the parts of the Body of Christ released in ministry. The model at the church of Antioch refreshingly pictures different ministries and gifts working together for a common purpose.

When Barnabas arrived from Jerusalem he soon saw fit to invite Saul to join him from Tarsus. They worked together in partnership and were soon joined by prophets (see Acts 11:27). Among them was Agabus, who predicted a famine in the Roman world. This led to gifts of help being sent to Judea. The team continued to grow, *'but Paul and Barnabas remained in Antioch, where they and many others taught and preached the word of the Lord'* (Acts 15:35).

In Acts 13 prophets and teachers are named and in the list there is evidence of people of differing nationalities and social order groups. Antioch has become a large apostolic centre ready to reach out into the world. This centre releases preachers, teachers and prophets and gives space for apologetics (in fending off legalism) and mercy ministries (see Acts 11:29).

There was both a variety and flexibility of ministry. I believe that the Church today would do well to examine this model if our world is to be affected. I agree wholeheartedly with the sentiments of Peter Wagner:

> 'We have moved into a season of the greatest outpouring of the power of the Holy Spirit and the greatest harvest of souls in all Christian history. Business as usual will not suffice in our churches and ministries today.'[2]

The vivid picture of the Church as the Body of Christ portrayed in 1 Corinthians 12 shows that every person in the Church is uniquely gifted. Surely our task today is to see the Church mobilised with every person motivated and released.

A church under enemy pressure

We would not do justice to the story of Antioch if we missed out this important aspect. The church was initiated out of persecution and in Acts 12:1–3 we see some arrested, James martyred and Peter imprisoned. I don't know why in God's plan there are those who lose their lives and others who are dramatically freed. I guess the church was praying for both Peter and James. The bottom line is that rebuilding temples is costly, and there is a price to pay. This message is underlined in Acts 14 with the words of the Apostles: *'We must go through many hardships to enter the kingdom of God'* (Acts 14:22). There remains a cost for all who want to push beyond mediocrity.

A church enjoying explosive growth

Out of the pain a powerful and growing community emerged becoming a 'sending church'. This involved releasing their best men:

> *'While they were worshipping the Lord and fasting, the Holy Spirit said, "Set apart for me Barnabas and Saul for the work to which I have called them."'* (Acts 13:2)

As they responded to the Holy Spirit the church began to grow. Reading the account in Acts it almost seems to come naturally:

> *' . . . a great number of people believed and turned to the Lord.'* (Acts 11:21)

> *' . . . a great number of people were brought to the Lord.'* (Acts 11:24)

> *' . . . taught great numbers of people.'* (Acts 11:26)

> *'But the word of God continued to increase and spread.'* (Acts 12:24)

Antioch was moving forward. As men and women were released in ministry, so its effectiveness and profile continued to grow.

> *'The word of the Lord spread through the whole region.'* (Acts 13:49)

Today, in various parts of the world, the Church is seeing great growth. At the beginning of the twentieth century there were hardly any believers in Korea, yet today, a number of the world's largest churches are in Seoul. We hear stories from Argentina, Singapore and various parts of Africa where explosive growth is taking place. In Lincoln, we are privileged to have John Phillips with us, and he is closely involved with the Assemblies of God in Brazil. He testifies of huge numbers regularly coming to Christ. However, in Britain we are still, generally speaking, seeing ones and twos coming to faith. It is in the heart of many of us to see things change and there are signs of hope. The DAWN movement has challenged our churches over recent years to consider 'planting' programmes again. New models of church are emerging and apostolic teams are increasingly focusing outward for the harvest.

Perhaps we need to recapture the urgency expressed by C.T. Studd in 1930:

> 'Let nobody mistake our objective, the Devil will seek to drag many red herrings across the scent. Our objective is the evangelising of the un-evangelised regions of the world.'[3]

I see today, as in the rebuilding of the temple in Ezra's day, the re-emergence of strong and effective churches taking a central position in society, with a heart that beats with a desire to reach the world.

Notes

1. Philip Yancey, *What's So Amazing About Grace* (Zondervan, 1997).
2. C. Peter Wagner from the foreword to *The Gift of Apostle* by David Cannistraci (Regal, 1996).
3. Patrick Johnstone, *The Church is Bigger Than You Think* (Christian Focus Publications/WEC, 1998).

Chapter 3

Rebuilding – the Walls

Moving from Ezra into Nehemiah, the picture of what is taking place enlarges. There is a very distinct movement from the spiritual life of the city to the city itself. Of course, to the Jewish mind, there was no distinction between the sacred and the secular as the entire city belonged to God. However, the challenge in British churches is to move beyond our small spiritual enclaves and out into the city. It is now time for the Church to make a difference. This can only take place through the mobilising of ordinary Christians who really care about their communities. Tragically, for too long, Christians have locked themselves away in their small inward-looking groups and have failed to engage with society. We need Christians who will care enough to be involved in every area of life. Our frontline troops are not the church leaders, vicars or pastors, but teachers, office workers, bankers, and hospital staff etc. The rebuilt walls symbolise the work that can be achieved as the Church becomes like salt scattered and light gathered. Nehemiah strategically works towards seeing the whole of Jerusalem affected.

▶ *The inspection of the wall*
Nehemiah's first task was to see how exactly the land lay. It was important that he adequately researched the state of the city and so, under the cover of darkness and with close friends attending, he inspected the walls. It was as he suspected:

> 'Then I said to them, "You see the trouble we are in: Jerusalem lies in ruins, and its gates have been burnt with fire." '
>
> (Nehemiah 2:17)

Today we are beginning to recognise how essential researching
an area is. When the Apostle Paul went to Athens he didn't just
start preaching in the market square but he gathered relevant
information that was going to help him engage with the people:

> *'For as I walked around and looked carefully at your objects of*
> *worship, I even found an altar with this inscription:* TO AN
> UNKNOWN GOD. *Now what you worship as something unknown I*
> *am going to proclaim to you.'*   (Acts 17:23)

Paul's research brought him keys for breakthrough in the city.

▶   **The building of the wall**

How was this going to be possible? Nehemiah begins to motivate
the people.

> *'Come, let us rebuild the wall of Jerusalem, and we will no longer*
> *be in disgrace.'*   (Nehemiah 2:17)

It could not possibly happen just with a personal agenda and
positive thinking. This would need to grip all the people. Everyone, whatever his or her gifts and abilities, would have to get
involved. They needed to understand that this was a *'good work'*
(Nehemiah 2:18) and that God would cause the impossible to
become possible. Nehemiah 3 names many people and groups of
people who gave themselves to the work. Priests and perfume-
makers that had not been used to manual labour became
involved and even goldsmiths were willing to get their hands
dirty.

▶   **A look at the builders**

Although these were ordinary people, Nehemiah managed to
motivate them and they made a start.

▶   **The people worked with all their hearts**

Throughout the Scriptures it is always the wholehearted that get
things done. This was to do with heart, soul and strength: *'for the*
people worked with all their heart' (Nehemiah 4:6). In the words of
Tommy Tenney: 'If a situation doesn't move you then you can't
move heaven.'[1]

▶ **The people worked near their homes**

Taking responsibility in our own homes and neighbourhoods is essential.

> *'Adjoining this, Jedaiah son of Harumaph made repairs opposite his own house.'* (Nehemiah 3:10)

I cannot imagine that anyone has heard of this character, or of his father, but he was part of God's answer. Our small contributions, when given to God and joined with others, really can make a difference.

▶ **The people worked with the help and protection of God**

In a day of broken relationships and fragmentation within the Body of Christ, we need to see what God can do when we lay down our personal agendas for the greater cause: *'but we prayed to our God'* (Nehemiah 4:9). They were conscious that *'the God of heaven will give us success'* (Nehemiah 2:20).

▶ **The people worked and warred**

Against a background of intense conflict, the people understood the spiritual warfare that they were involved in. This meant increased levels of vigilance and readiness.

> *'Those who carried materials did their work with one hand and held a weapon in the other, and each of the builders wore his sword at his side as he worked.'* (Nehemiah 4:17–18)

Seeing our cities impacted will need increased levels of prayer, unity and vigilance.

▶ **The people worked with persistence and focus**

Once the start was made there was no turning back. Though ridiculed and threatened, the workers kept moving on. It was not comfortable and high commitment levels were essential.

> *'Neither I nor my brothers nor my men nor the guards with me took off our clothes; each had his weapon, even when he went for water.'* (Nehemiah 4:23)

This was twenty-four hours, seven days a week devotion to God. I must confess that it would be easy to get discouraged with waning commitment levels where, for some, even attending Sunday worship is a struggle. However, leaders need to lead, and the bottom line is 'it is the Lord who provides the enthusiasm by His Spirit'.

As progress was being made negative voices began to increase. I naively thought in the past that if we sought to do good things we would gain approval, and particularly approval from the Christian community. However, trying to live godly lives will always bring opposition. As the people began the building two negative voices could clearly be heard:

- **It's impossible!** This was the contribution of Sanballat: *'Can they bring the stones back to life from those heaps of rubble?'* (Nehemiah 4:2). In the natural, after seventy years of inactivity, it seemed highly unlikely there would be much change. This negative declaration still affects most Christian communities today, and even believers think major change is highly unlikely.

- **It's ineffective!** Tobiah, another 'positive' brother, said that even if the wall went up it would hardly be strong enough to hold back future armies. Tobiah the Ammonite, who was at Sanballat's side (negative attracts negative) said, *'What they are building – if even a fox climbed up on it, he would break down their wall of stones!'* (Nehemiah 4:3). Many churches still, unfortunately, have helpful counsellors like Tobiah! We need to break the thought from our churches that nothing will ever really change. The rebuilding of walls is not easy either, especially when you're standing in rubble.

► *Rubble can dishearten*

Looking at the leftovers of past movements of God can put us off any rebuilding. Reading of the great things of past years can, if we are not careful, create a sense of disillusionment. Stories of miracles, or men and women of faith in days gone by, can cause some to be tempted to give up.

► *Rubble can delay*

Some of the workers were becoming so tired removing debris and dust that it seemed as though all their attention was given to clearing up, rather than moving on. However, the rubble must be removed and the foundations of new walls reset. Thankfully, we find ourselves often building on the old foundations or, to change the analogy, re-digging ancient wells.

▶ **The completion of the wall**
'So the wall was completed on the twenty-fifth of Elul, in fifty-two days.' (Nehemiah 6:15)

This is one of the most remarkable verses in Scripture. Against all the odds the vision of Nehemiah became a reality. The enemies around recognised that this was not a human achievement but was because of the help of the Lord. Sometimes God's timings are amazing. For some things it seems God's 'quickly' or 'soon' is incredibly slow from our human perspective, but on this occasion, His 'quick' is quick. It all happened in fifty-two days. In my own ministry I have been aware of some things taking so long to get into place. I fear that the walls of Jerusalem may not even have got onto our leaders' meeting agenda in fifty-two days.

The story of rebuilt walls challenges us to see the mobilisation of the whole Church. Every person is gifted and has a contribution to make. Our living faith in Jesus should energise us to do the things that will please Him. Reaching cities will require Christian influence running through education, health, the pop industry, politics and the police, expressing itself in genuine love for the hurting and marginalized. Recently, we have begun to see many examples of living faith in action. One such initiative is *Faithworks*, with Steve Chalke, where many stories are being shared of churches making a difference to the very walls of cities. Sandy Miller, the vicar of Holy Trinity, Brompton, in the foreword to *Faithworks 2* by Steve Chalke, writes:

> 'I cannot remember a time when it was so urgent for the church of Jesus Christ in all its rich variety, to pull together to demonstrate the love of God in the practical work of compassion and service, and I am convinced that the recent outpouring of God's Spirit has inspired many new initiatives and individuals in renewed acts of kindness and self-sacrifice. It is extremely encouraging, though we have a long way to go.'[2]

Incidentally, may God bless Delirious, who are not just content entertaining the Christian troops, but are eager to carve out a path into the wider music scene. May it be that a new generation of history-makers are let loose into our cities.

Notes
1. Tommy Tenney, *God's Secret to Greatness* (Regal Books, 2000), p. 68.
2. Steve Chalke, *Faithworks 2: Stories of Hope* (Kingsway Publications, 2001).

Chapter 4

Rebuilding – the Setting

God has amazing ways of bringing things together at the right time. He always sets the scene and prepares people and situations in order that His plans find fulfilment. When God sent His Son into the world, it was at exactly the right time and the arranging of a Roman census so that Bethlehem should be the birthplace, as foretold by the prophets, was of no problem to Him. In the days of Ezra and Nehemiah, God brought everything together and, after many barren years, something new was about to break.

New things emerge

Envisioned leaders
There had been a dearth of leadership in the land for a long time. Yet, as the first page of the book of Ezra is turned, God raises up a leader from a very unexpected source. In the first year of Cyrus, king of Persia, the Lord *'moved'* his heart. A pagan king suddenly began to be moved upon. He knew there was an emerging call upon his life, so much so that he delivered an edict concerning the rebuilding of the temple at Jerusalem and declared: *'he has appointed me to build a temple for him at Jerusalem in Judea'* (Ezra 1:2). Nobody would have expected leadership to come to God's people from this pagan king. However, this was part of God's sovereign plan. His emergence had been prophesied by Jeremiah years before (see 2 Chronicles 36:22). The scene was being set. Zerubbabel, Joshua and Nehemiah were also standing in the wings ready to respond to God's call of leadership upon their lives. These were to be leaders of initiative and vision who would

bring motivation and direction to God's people. God was assigning specific leadership tasks. Men of differing gifts and abilities were being raised up. Zerubbabel provided administrative strength, Ezra solid scriptural foundations and Nehemiah charismatic, motivational leadership. Clearly there was a sovereign hand behind these events. There is something very liberating in the statement expressed by John the Baptist when he said, *'A man can receive only what is given him from heaven'* (John 3:27). There is a great need for leaders today to move in their allotted spheres of gifting. We also need to be aware that when God's call is upon people, they won't necessarily come from the places we expect. They may not emerge from Bible colleges or even Christian backgrounds. Perhaps we need to recognise a new breed of leadership who have differing ways of operating. We need to recognise the call and anointing of God. Like Samuel, we can make our choices based on outward appearances and leave the anointed leader out in the fields of obscurity. However, God has His ways of setting the scene. As leadership began to take its place, another important factor came into being.

Willing people

Having touched the heart of Cyrus, God also begins to bring hope to the people. As the edict is released new levels of responsiveness emerge. Families begin to respond to the possibilities of rebuilding the temple and prepare to move territory. Everyone whose heart God has moved, prepares to go up and build the house of the Lord in Jerusalem (see Ezra 1:5).

▶   *They were willing to work*

Much work was necessary in preparing to go home. With the help of neighbours and friends, materials and livestock were gathered together and preparations were made.

▶   *They were willing to give*

Large amounts of finance were found as *'freewill offerings towards the building of the house of God on its site'* (Ezra 2:68), were made. Giving is always a sign of renewal.

▶   *They were willing to learn*

When eventually the time came for Ezra to remind the people of who they were and as the book of the Law was publicly read, the

Bible says, *'all the people listened attentively'* (Nehemiah 8:3). A new sensitivity was emerging in God's people. They wanted to hear God's Word and be willing in the day of His power.

▶ **They were willing to respond**
Having listened, the people began to do what is written. They faced the challenges that the Word had brought and began to make adjustments with regard to their lifestyles. Many had intermarried with other nations and they responded by changing their behaviour.

There are two interesting verses in the Song of Deborah in Judges 5 that highlight the importance of both effective leadership and willing people:

> *'When the princes in Israel take the lead,*
>   *when the people willingly offer themselves –*
>   *praise the LORD!'*   (Judges 5:2)

> *'My heart is with Israel's princes,*
>   *with the willing volunteers among the people.*
>   *Praise the LORD!'*   (Judges 5:9)

The above verses can be read with a different emphasis and intonation. As a pastor I find myself emphasising after a sharp intake of breath, *'Praise the Lord!'* It is a great blessing, and also a relief, when leaders lead and people willingly follow.

Supportive Ministries
We have already begun to consider the different gifts and abilities of the new leaders, but it is also worth noting the attitudes of the prophets to what was taking place. It is not always the case that 'builders' and 'prophets' see eye to eye, but each gift endorses and blesses the other: *'And the prophets of God were with them, helping them'* (Ezra 5:2).

Zechariah and Haggai spoke words of affirmation to Zerubbabel, Joshua and the team. Though there were great obstacles ahead, the promise was:

> *'What are you, O mighty mountain? Before Zerubbabel you will become level ground. Then he will bring out the capstone to shouts of "God bless it! God bless it!"'*   (Zechariah 4:7)

It is essential in today's church that ministries endorse, bless and release one another. It is so important for builders and prophets to sing from the same hymn sheet.

Strength in opposition

Any genuine work of God will always be opposed, but the thing that stands out in this account is the strength that God brought. He seemed to give a special 'overcoming spirit' to the leadership team. I recently studied the letters of Jesus to the churches in Revelation and was intrigued to find in each letter references to 'overcoming'. I found that the phrase, *'to him who overcomes'* is found in Revelation 2:7, 11, 17, 26, and in Revelation 3:5, 11, 21. This need to 'overcome' is important for each church. On further examination I found a link between 'overcoming' and three things:

1. **Hearing** (Revelation 2:7, 11, 17 and 3:20)
2. **Holding** (Revelation 2:25 and 3:11)
3. **Holiness** (Revelation 3:4)

Overcoming clearly has to do with hearing a word from God, holding on to that word whatever happens and living a life of integrity and holiness. These three things seem to fit our story. Ezra and Nehemiah, having heard from God, held on to that word and pressed through to its completion. To be honest to the text, we must spend some time looking at the pressures they faced. To be 'over-comers' implies there will be much to over-come. Without the favour of God it is unlikely that Ezra and Nehemiah would have made it but they certainly became 'more than conquerors'.

Ezra 4 is filled with all kinds of opposition. Within two verses we find three enemies that most of us, as Christians, will have to face:

> *'Then the peoples around them set out to **discourage** the people of Judah and make them **afraid** to go on building. They hired counsellors to work against them and **frustrate** their plans ... '*
> (Ezra 4:4–5)

How often have we sought to build something of value for God and been faced with discouragement, fear and frustration.

Ezra 4:7 alludes to *'a letter'*. Without spending too much time on this weapon I would just say that they usually appear in brown envelopes with the words 'Private and Confidential' emblazoned on the front in large letters. I remember receiving one of these 'missiles' a few minutes before the Sunday morning service. Everything in me was suggesting that I shouldn't open the envelope before the meeting but curiosity got the better of me. After all, it could be a cheque, or a letter of thanks from one of our members, or maybe a helpful, uplifting and edifying prophecy that would propel me onto the platform with a great sense of zeal and faith. However, to my surprise (not!) the letter informed me that 'I have built on sand and great would be the fall of the house.' This was endorsed by a multitude of verses from the Minor Prophets, written in red ink for greater effect and impact. Though I knew the source of the letter was spurious, I felt life draining from me and looked up to the ceiling of our building to see if the cracks had started to emerge. The pain of this encounter was re-awakened a few days later with a knock on the door. A smartly dressed gentleman informed me he had 'a word from the Lord for me'. This man's appearance and his rich Scottish accent gave a sense of credibility and I nervously asked him if it was 'a good one'. 'I'm only the postman,' he replied. I caught sight of my wife, Irene, in the corner of my eye. She was out of view of the man in question, but was rigorously shaking her head in a way that made it clear I should not receive this word. However, I thought this could be the Lord, and the man did look 'prophetic', so the word was delivered: 'You have built on sand and great will be the fall of the house.' Without even saying, 'have a nice day' he left. I turned around to see if there was some kind of solace and consolation from Irene, but she was in the kitchen washing the pots, as though nothing had happened. When I asked if she had heard the delivered 'word', she replied, 'Yes. I think he was a friend of the person who sent the "confidential" letter.' And so he was. Thank God for a wife who is able to interpret and discern missiles. Make no mistake, simple 'letters' can be highly debilitating and can rob us of our peace.

In Ezra 4 we see the **delay** tactics of *'standstill'*.

> *'Thus the work on the house of God in Jerusalem came to a standstill until the second year of the reign of Darius king of Persia.'*   (Ezra 4:24)

We have often found frustration through delay. Most charismatic leaders are looking for things to happen **now**. It is important to say that 'standstill' doesn't mean that things are over. It simply means that we may have to wait a little longer.

In Nehemiah the catalogue of enemy opposition increases. The following list gives us a sense of the size of the battle:

• Angry, incensed, ridiculed (Nehemiah 4:1)

• Ridicule (Nehemiah 4:3)

• Very angry (Nehemiah 4:7)

• Plot (Nehemiah 4:8)

• Exaggeration (Nehemiah 4:12)

• Intimidation (Nehemiah 6:13)

• False prophecy (Nehemiah 6:14)

So often the enemy suggests that what we are doing is worthless and will prove to be ineffective. There is often the 'enemy within', when people close to us question, challenge or even leave us. There is also 'the enemy without' where we face the Sanballats and Tobiahs who just want to see us fail. We need to arm ourselves with God's Word, hold on to what He says and try to live lives worthy of our calling in the best way we know how. God was setting the scene and putting everything in place. Today, God wants to see the leaders emerging who will lead His willing people into a place of victory. There will be opposition but His strength is with us, and with a little help from our friends we will see things rebuilt for His glory.

Chapter 5

Rebuilding – the Breakout

In order for rebuilding to take place, it is important that there is a breaking out of the status quo. New levels of passion and commitment are necessary, together with new concepts of leadership. In the days of Ezra and Nehemiah, God's people experienced 'breakout', as Nehemiah began to discover a God-given burden.

Breakout in Nehemiah's day

He received a burden
Verse 1 of Nehemiah introduces us to Nehemiah the Son of Hachaliah (whom Jehovah disturbs). It is not uncommon for those who find themselves on the stage of God's appointing to be in the faith trail of those who have gone before. When Solomon built the temple, he was fulfilling the promises given to his father, David. It seems to me that Nehemiah (Jehovah comforts) was made ready by God to receive a burden, as Hanani (Jehovah gave) brings important information:

> *'The wall of Jerusalem is broken down, and its gates have been burned with fire.'* (Nehemiah 1:3)

To a homesick Jew this was news that caused a deep level of emotional and spiritual response. The dictionary defines a 'burden' as 'something heavy that is carried'. A weight descended upon Nehemiah. Paul Scanlon of Abundant Life Centre, Bradford, writes: 'Many people in the church are lifting and shifting but not carrying.'[1] It is my belief that those who carry the weight are the ones who should shape the church. Information received into a prepared heart can become a burden.

He took the burden back to God

When God has placed something into your hands have you ever thought, 'What do I do with this?' Nehemiah, on receiving the burden, took it straight back to God in prayer:

> *'I sat down and wept. For some days I mourned and fasted and prayed before the God of heaven.'*   (Nehemiah 1:4)

In his prayers a number of things took place:

▶ **He acknowledged God's sovereignty** (Nehemiah 1:5)
When burdens come our way it's important to know that God is in charge.

▶ **He identified with Israel's sins** (Nehemiah 1:6–7)
There is a lot of emphasis today in certain parts of the Church on 'intercessory identification' and, without entering too much into the debate, it is clear that Nehemiah identified with the sins of those who had gone before. It is always healthy to pray 'we' and not 'their' prayers.

▶ **He pleaded God's covenant promises** (Nehemiah 1:8–9)
God had not forgotten His promises concerning Israel, but disobedience had held back the blessing.

▶ **He prayed for success** (Nehemiah 1:11)
This was a clear and a strong prayer, which meant that he knew when it was answered. Sometimes our prayers are so vague that we leave different options for God, so that we are not too disappointed. We don't know exactly how long Nehemiah prayed but it seems that throughout this process he just kept doing the things that he needed to do. On a very ordinary working day he did what he always did, but suddenly a door of opportunity opened. As he took wine to King Artaxerxes the burden that had been carried secretly in his heart began to manifest in his appearance: *'Why does your face look so sad when you're not ill?'* (Nehemiah 2:2). This was a fearful question as cupbearers who didn't smile in the king's presence could

permanently lose their smile, as their heads were removed. The next question was even more incredible: *'What is it you want?'* (Nehemiah 2:4). There was, perhaps, an instant desire to feign madness, as David had done, to gain some time for thought, but instead he threw up one of the most common types of prayer known to man: *'Then I prayed to the God of heaven'* (Nehemiah 2:4). Scripture doesn't enlighten us to what was said but I'm sure it could be summed up in the short, panic-stricken word, '**Help!**' The gracious hand of the Lord was now opening the door of opportunity that had been prayed for.

He let the burden take shape
The king amazingly responded to all the requests made by Nehemiah. Not only was he free to go to Jerusalem to see what he could do, but he was also given protection for the journey and royal letters that would give him access where it was needed. The first thing that became necessary when he entered Jerusalem was **investigation**. He didn't just take people's word for it but systematically and carefully looked at the condition of the fallen city. As we work towards seeing rebuilding take place, research of what is the real situation is essential. He then moved towards **strategy** and **focus**. When God gives us a burden, focus is essential. Some time ago, I felt God challenge my heart with the words 'set your face like flint'. I have not always found it easy to keep focused and have a tendency to stray off course or get diverted. Intrigued by this word, I looked up the word 'flint' in the dictionary and found it was 'a hard stone, shaped for purpose'. As the burden takes shape there is no doubt in my mind that we are also being shaped, so that God can trust us with what He has given us. Jerusalem had lain in ruins for one hundred and twenty years and desperately needed 'breakout'.

He shared the burden with others
It was now time for **motivation**. Nehemiah shares his burden with others and begins to build a team of willing people:

> *'Come, let us rebuild the wall of Jerusalem, and we will no longer be in disgrace.'* (Nehemiah 2:17)

In his book *Taking Our Cities for God* John Dawson writes, 'God organises His Kingdom through gifts of friendship'.[2] We were never designed to carry the load by ourselves. Later, we will examine the New Testament picture of apostolic ministry, which constantly seeks to break into new territory. The apostle Paul, as a master builder, is determined to see new communities of faith planted, but it is important to note at this time, that he never did it alone. John Maxwell in *The 21 Most Powerful Minutes in a Leader's Day* writes:

> 'In the early years after his conversion, Paul spent time alone. Like many other biblical leaders, he was labouring in obscurity to be prepared to fulfil his calling. But once he travelled to Jerusalem for the first time and began leading others and planting churches, he never worked alone again. Everywhere he went, he took companions.'[3]

Nehemiah worked alongside Ezra, Zerubbabel and Jeshua, with a host of ordinary people joining the workforce also.

He saw the burden fulfil its potential

What an amazing story. After King Artaxerxes provided an open door of opportunity it wasn't long before gates were re-established (see Nehemiah 3), opposition was overcome (Nehemiah 4), the poor were helped (Nehemiah 5), the wall was completed (Nehemiah 6), and the people praised again (Nehemiah 12). The city became a different place because a man picked up God's burden.

Let us look at 'the apostolic'. In the last few years there has been much interest in this subject. Less people today are clinging to the belief that apostolic ministry came to a close, following the death of the twelve, or thirteen if you count Matthias, or even fourteen if you count Paul. I have often felt sorry for Joseph, known as Justus, who no doubt became known as the man who nearly made it through. He must have had similar qualities to the others, even to make the shortlist.

The emergence of apostolic vision

In the rebuilding in today's church I believe apostolic ministries need to emerge. We need to push through from the nostalgic to the prophetic, from being heritage-driven to being vision-driven. The following may be helpful to illustrate that the apostolic is earthed in reality and, if released, will cause a 'breakout'. Apostolic vision will:

1. Require church leaders who know how to focus
Already we have majored on the importance of leaders emerging who can move the church forward. Paul used the phrase, *'but one thing I do'* (Philippians 3:13). In the multiplicity of options, in today's 'pick and mix' spirituality, we need leaders who know they have been given something from God to carry that will make a difference. They are leaders who are marked out by faith and patience.

2. Recognise the church needs to be built relationally
In 2 Corinthians 6, Paul emphasised to the Corinthian church the importance of strong relationships. He implores this divided community to learn the art of open communication:

> *'We have spoken freely to you, Corinthians, and opened wide our hearts to you.'*   (2 Corinthians 6:11)

Paul was not just a strategic thinker but he also knew the value of two-way communication at heart level.

> *'We are not withholding our affection from you, but you are withholding yours from us.'*   (2 Corinthians 6:12)

Have you ever been in a situation where you have opened your heart in the presence of friends, only to face a period of awkward silence? Paul says:

> *'As a fair exchange – I speak as to my children – open wide your hearts also.'*   (2 Corinthians 6:13)

As a father to the church, Paul encourages the church to relate at a deeper and more vulnerable level. This begins to deal with the veneer and releases realistic relationships of friendship and loyalty that will make sure the job gets done.

3. Prepare the Church to contend for the faith
Some time ago I was looking for material to bring to younger leaders and studied what we often call the 'pastoral epistles'. During this fresh look at 1 and 2 Timothy and Titus, I was

surprised to see all of the battles that these emerging ministries were facing. False doctrines, myths, endless genealogies, controversies, shipwrecked-faith, old wives tales and teaching spreading like gangrene – these give us a slightly different perception of the early Church. It was into this environment that Paul addresses his spiritual sons with words of encouragement and challenge. He writes:

> *'Fight the good fight of the faith. Take hold of the eternal life to which you were called.'*   (1 Timothy 6:12)

The Church needs to know that we may not be whisked out of trouble, but we may have to contend for the faith.

4. Rely on the supernatural power of God
In order for 'breakout' to take place, a level of supernatural power needs to emerge in the Church. Our Western mindset has often limited the miraculous, which is either locked into past historic stories and anecdotes, or revivals in other parts of the world. Don Williams in his book *Signs, Wonders and the Kingdom of God* writes:

> 'My theological education provided me with a system of doctrine with which to control my faith, exegetical roots with which to control the Bible, management tools with which to control the church, and counselling techniques with which to control the people.'[4]

He then met John Wimber and as a result, his mindset began to change.

Recently, whilst on holiday in Yorkshire, Irene and I visited a graveyard – not usually what we do for recreation – just outside Bradford, where we found the grave of Smith Wigglesworth. Seeing this plot of land, we were challenged by his openness to the power of the Holy Spirit. Perhaps there needs to be a re-emergence of 'apostles of faith' who will press beyond normal church borders, in order to see the Kingdom come.

5. Present the Church with the possibility of unity
Apostolic ministry, in the words of Gerald Coates, is about 'raiding the future'.[5] It sees a day that is not yet with us. It has

a view of a church that is yet to come. It sees the possibility of unity within the church. Psalm 133 pictures what happens when people *'live together in unity'* (Psalm 133:1). This is more than ecumenical get-togethers – it is about 'dwelling' together. When this genuine, God-given unity emerges it is like 'oil' and it is like 'dew'. Both of these images are closely connected with the Holy Spirit. The psalmist sees something coming down. Check in the psalm how often the word 'down' occurs. Charles Spurgeon writes: 'Its way is downward'.[6] In our day, we need something special to come down from heaven that will pull us from our small agendas, into the bigger plans and purposes of God for villages, towns, cities, regions and even nations.

> I've been washing my nets for too long
> On the shores of unbelief
> Listening through hours of meetings
> Now it's time to do what I see
> To put out into deeper water
> Sail away on the winds of faith
> I see there's a massive harvest
> The nets will almost break . . .
>
> Breakout! This is the time to
> Breakout! This is the call to
> Breakout! This is the year of the breakout . . .
>
> Keep pressing in and forget the old thing
> See the new thing springing up
> New wine for a brand new wineskin
> Fresh oil with an ancient touch
> Make room for the great awakening
> It's here and it's on its way
> We'll see God's kingdom break out
> To the right and the left today.
>
> It's time to call to the shore
> We'll need some partners . . .
> It's time to ask the Lord
> To send more labourers.
>
> (© Godfrey Birtill & Dale Gentry, 2001)[7]

Notes

1. Paul Scanlon, *God's Fingerprint* (Hodder and Stoughton, 1999).
2. John Dawson, *Taking Our Cities for God* (Creation House, 2001).

3. John Maxwell, *The 21 Most Powerful Minutes in a Leader's Day* (Thomas Nelson, 2000).
4. Don Williams, *Signs, Wonders and the Kingdom of God* (Vine Books, 1989).
5. Gerald Coates from a spoken message entitled 'Raiding the Future' at Grapevine conference, 1985.
6. C.H. Spurgeon, *Great Verses from the Psalms: Selections from the Treasury of David* (Zondervan).
7. Godfrey Birtill, Whitefield Music, Fertile Ground, PO Box 77, Hailsham, East Sussex. Used by permission.

Chapter 6

Rebuilding – the Gates

Many in church leadership desire level ground or a clean sheet. So often leaders feel 'hemmed in' by expectations, traditions or red tape. Before the gates could be put in place, the remnant of yesterday's walls needed to be removed.

More rubble Zerrubabel

> 'The strength of the labourers is giving out, and there is so much rubble that we cannot rebuild the wall.'   (Nehemiah 4:10)

Yesterday's walls so often become today's rubble. Good things that served God's purposes faithfully in the past need to be removed. This is never easy, especially if there is a memorial plaque attached to the old wall, with the name of a faithful church member of the past who, with great sacrifice, had given to the cause. However, the truth is that the sensitive use of 'prayed over' wheelbarrows is essential to give space for the new building to emerge. In reality, we can only be faithful to obediently pursue what God is telling us to contribute within our lifetime; others must stand in the gap for the generations that are yet to come. The words 'we've always done it this way' must be replaced by, 'Lord, what would you have me to do!'

Far too many leaders find themselves 'sifting' the rubble rather than 'serving' the Kingdom. The frustration of red tape, denominationalism, constitutions and traditions can delay the rebuilding. At this point it would be useful to find an Old Testament map of Jerusalem in the days of Nehemiah. We are going to visit each gate and follow the wall round the city. It is worth remembering that a city without walls was a city cursed. In a similar way, we need to see today's church as a city blessed by the Lord. For me, as I look at the re-emergence of the walls and gates of the old Jerusalem, I see a picture begin to take shape of an apostolic church. Each gate represents an essential characteristic of today's church, the alternative God-empowered community.

The Sheep Gate (Nehemiah 3:1)

This was the starting point. Amazingly, from within the religious structure of the day, the programme begins. Eliashib (whom Jehovah restores) the high priest, sets things in motion. It was highly significant that this gate was prioritised as the place to start. This was the gate through which sacrificial lambs were bought to the temple mount. Nehemiah knew that the sacrificial system within the city should begin again, in order that spiritual issues should be at the heart of all rebuilding.

In terms of a New Testament picture of church, it is essential that this gate be put in place again. Jesus is *'the Lamb of God, who takes away the sin of the world'* (John 1:29), and the one supreme sacrifice, for all people, for all time. In any restoration of church life, the finished work of Jesus Christ on the cross must be our priority. Through the years, the fires of liberal theology have destroyed this gate. The cross of Christ remains our rebuilding starting point.

The Fish Gate (Nehemiah 3:3)

The next gate to be put in place was the Fish Gate. This was the gate through which fish would once again be brought to the markets of Jerusalem from the Mediterranean and the Sea of Galilee. A new economic life of market activity would bring the sounds of life back to the city, which had lain in ruins for too long.

The sign of the fish has been a sign of the Christian faith since the days of the early Church. In terms of an apostolic church, the faith that has been received must be passed on. Christ's words to Peter, *'I will make you fishers of men'* (Mark 1:17), have become a motto for evangelism. We are called to proclaim the gospel in word and deed. A healthy church will consistently be looking to catch fish. Evangelism must again be at the heart of our communities.

Old (Jeshanah) Gate (Nehemiah 3:6)

This is the gate that links the old part of the city with the new. Nehemiah knew that Jerusalem needed a sense of identity in its incredible history and that it must not have forgotten its roots. The city was to serve the God of Abraham, Isaac and Jacob.

This is important for the church today. In our rebuilding work, we need to establish an 'old gate'. In some quarters there is a crazy notion that everything old is bad. We must remember the host of witnesses who have gone before us. We need to re-dig the ancient walls and re-walk the ancient paths. Our roots need to firmly recognise and honour that which has gone before. A wise scribe still brings out of his storehouse both the new and the old.

Valley Gate (Nehemiah 3:13)

On the southern slopes, outside the walls of Jerusalem, spreads the valley of Hinnom. This valley highlighted the darker side of Israel's history, for it was in this valley that children were sacrificed to Molech as they were offered for the fire (see 2 Kings 23:10). Gates are for opening and for closing. The Valley Gate remained a constant reminder of this idolatrous past.

Again, in today's church, the 'valley gate' should be closed and bolted and a sign erected 'No idolatry here!' All idolatry and the serving of other gods needs to be kept out of the city. This church needs to be clean, and the only fire that should burn within her walls should be the fire of the Holy Spirit.

Dung Gate (Nehemiah 3:14)

No prizes for guessing the use of this gate. Yes, you have it. This was the gate outside of which all the human refuse and the rubbish of the city was tipped. Needless to say, this was not the most sought after area of the city to live in. However, this area was essential for good sanitation and a healthy environment.

In the church we need to build a 'dung gate', where we say that all that speaks of human ability, effort and ambition should be outside the city. In fact, Paul counted all his human expertise and learning as *'rubbish, that I may gain Christ'* (Philippians 3:8). 'Rubbish' is translated as *dung* in the Authorised Version.

Fountain Gate (Nehemiah 3:15)

This area was more upmarket. It was a place of refreshment, close to the pool of Siloam. On reading about this gate I was

automatically reminded of the need for a Fountain Gate in our
churches today. This speaks to me of the work of the Holy Spirit
that Jesus promised would spring up from within us. Today's
church desperately needs the Holy Spirit. I am deeply grateful to
God for those who helped me through the years to discover this
gate. I am committed to seeing a church where the Holy Spirit is
made welcome and where seasons of refreshing come to us from
the hand of the Lord.

Water Gate (Nehemiah 3:26)

No scandal here. This gate, close to the virgin springs, was the
gate through which water was brought into the city. A healthy
city needs a good, clean, water supply. From the days of
Hezekiah emphasis was laid on the importance of an adequate
water supply for Jerusalem.

To me, it is significant that the Fountain Gate stands next to
the Water Gate. As the Fountain Gate speaks of the Holy Spirit,
so the Water Gate speaks of the Word of God. There are many
references to 'water' and 'the word' in the Scriptures, but how
interesting that, when Ezra rises up to proclaim the 'Word of
God', he does so standing in front of the Water Gate:

> *'All the people assembled as one man in a square before the
> Water Gate. They told Ezra the scribe to bring out the Book of the
> Law of Moses.'*   (Nehemiah 8:1)

The Spirit and the Word need to come together in a restored
church of strength and life.

Horse Gate (Nehemiah 3:28)

This gate was designed for battle. Nehemiah recognised that
Jerusalem needed to be secure. It must not again be overthrown
by the enemy and must have been able to defend its citizens.

Today's church needs to recognise the reality of spiritual
warfare. Its battle is not with 'flesh and blood', and its cry is
'the battle belongs to the Lord.' For too long the church has
retreated. It is called to advance, and the promise is that the gates
of hell will not prevail against it.

East Gate (Nehemiah 3:29)

Some years ago, on a visit to the Holy Land, I spent some time
looking at the old East Gate. It was no longer a place of access.

Concrete blocked the entrance, and Muslim graves covered the threshold. Recognising this to be the Messiah's Gate, I was aware that His entrance to the golden city was being challenged. Nehemiah prepared the gate through which Jesus would, at a future date, enter the city. Today's East Gate points to the fact that this same Jesus, at a future date, would return in power and glory.

What then does this gate signify for us today? Simply this: Jesus is the Lord of the Church, He is head of the body. He is King of kings and Lord of lords. Like the early Church our declaration should be 'Jesus Christ is Lord!'

Inspection Gate (Nehemiah 3:31)

At this restored gate, when the trumpet sounded, the people would gather. It was also known as the Muster Gate. This was the gate where everyone recognised that they were called to be citizens of Jerusalem. They would stand together when opposed and find a common identity, standing shoulder to shoulder, with a sense of pride in who they were.

This gate reminds me of the importance of unity. There is a call for God's people to 'muster', to stand together and identify themselves, not in terms of denomination or preference but as fellow Christians on a life-changing journey together.

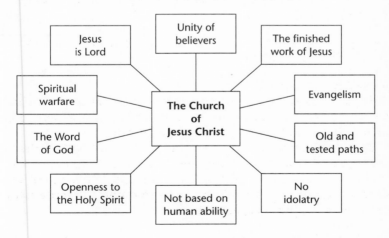

Chapter 7

Rebuilding – the Purpose

God had a purpose for Jerusalem and for Jerusalem's people. Ezra begins with the Word of the Lord. It was in God's heart for His city to be rebuilt. In Jeremiah 25 we read of a prophecy that warned the people of God of a coming calamity:

> ' "I will summon all the peoples of the north and my servant Nebuchadnezzar king of Babylon," declares the LORD, "and I will bring them against this land and its inhabitants and against all the surrounding nations. I will completely destroy them and make them an object of horror and scorn, and an everlasting ruin." '
>
> (Jeremiah 25:9)

Behind this story was a providential hand and God's clock was to tick for another seventy years before the edict of Cyrus heralded a new day. God was working out His purposes for His special city. The time of judgement would be followed by a time of blessing.

It is good to know that there is a hand overseeing history. Throughout the book of Ezra the Lord is seen to be sovereign over all kingdoms, even to raising up a pagan king to lead when He sees fit. It is God who stirs the hearts of the people and raises leadership. However, God is looking for the ready and willing in every generation. He is not a divine puppeteer pulling on the strings of humanity but gives men and women the gift of choice and a free will. Every generation needs its Ezras and Nehemiahs.

Plans for hope

Jeremiah points to a rebuilding day beyond the destruction:

> *'When seventy years are completed for Babylon, I will come to you and fulfil my gracious promise to bring you back to this place.'*
> (Jeremiah 29:10)

God's purpose ultimately is never breakdown and judgement. He always wants plans to come to pass that will bring prosperity. He offers *'plans to give you hope and a future'* (Jeremiah 29:11). Jerusalem was not intended to be desolate but to be populated with praising people.

Jerusalem – the Golden City

The Scriptures lay out God's purposes for Jerusalem from Genesis to Revelation.

Its name

- Jerusalem (Peace)
- City of God (Psalm 46:4)
- Zion (1 Kings 8:1)
- City of the Great King (Psalm 48:2)
- City of David (2 Samuel 5:7)
- City of Judah (2 Chronicles 25:28)
- Ariel (Isaiah 29:1)
- The joy of the whole earth (Lamentations 2:15)
- Holy City (Nehemiah 11:1)
- The throne of the Lord (Jeremiah 3:17)
- City of Truth (Zechariah 8:3)
- Holy Mountain (Daniel 9:16)

These many names show us the great value that God placed in this middle-east geography.

Its situation

> *'Jerusalem is built like a city*
> *that is closely compacted together.*
> *That is where the tribes go up,*
> *the tribes of the LORD,*
> *to praise the name of the LORD.'*   (Psalm 122:3–4)

> *'As the mountains surround Jerusalem,*
> *so the LORD surrounds his people*
> *both now and for evermore.'*   (Psalm 125:2)

> *'You are beautiful, my darling, as Tirzah,*
> *lovely as Jerusalem,*
> *majestic as troops with banners.'*   (Song of Songs 6:4)

> *'As for you, O watchtower of the flock,*
> *O stronghold of the Daughter of Zion,*
> *the former dominion will be restored to you;*
> *kingship will come to the Daughter of Jerusalem.'*
>   .   (Micah 4:8)

These verses show how highly Jerusalem is regarded in the purposes of God. It is a place of safety, a place for the gathering of God's people; a place of beauty and a place of strength.

In 1982, I led our fellowship on a cut-price holiday to Israel. We decided to stay in a kibbutz rather than a hotel and tried to avoid the usual tourist trappings. Our guide encouraged us to make an early morning visit to the Mount of Olives so that we could watch the rising of the sun strike the domes and yellow buildings of the city. When we left for the trip the skies were cloudy but as the sun broke through we saw it shine on the 'golden city'. This was a sight never to be forgotten.

Its influence

Through history this one city has been at the centre of much activity. Throughout the Bible years, Jerusalem had been attacked and captured by Shishak, king of Egypt (1 Kings 14:26), Jehoash, king of Israel (2 Kings 14:13), Nebuchadnezzar, king of Babylon, followed by Antiochus Epiphanes (2 Kings 24:8–16), Manasseh (2 Chronicles 33:14), Pekah (2 Kings 16:5), the Philistines (2 Chronicles 21:16–17) and Sennacherib (2 Kings 18:13–37), to name but a few.

Up until modern times armies have come and gone and for Jerusalem, such a small city, its influence has been so great. Not only has there been conflict against the city but also conflict within her walls. The temple mount remains a point of contention between Jews and Arabs as Jews pray at the Wailing Wall and Muslims gather in the Al-Aqsa Mosque.

Perhaps the 'peace of Jerusalem' has consistently been under threat because the story of God's dealings with His people has taken place on this chosen real estate. From the mysterious Melchizedek to the servant King David, from captain Joshua and the army of Israel to the splendours of Solomon, Jerusalem has been at the centre of God's purposes. Yet the greatest story ever told focuses on the man of heaven who set His face like flint to die upon a cross outside this city's walls. Little did Ezra and Nehemiah realise that this city and its walls were crucial to an eternal plan worked out before the foundation of the world.

Its destiny

It was from an upper room in this city's catchments area that a wind blew that was to change the world forever. The Holy Spirit came to a small group that were seeking humanity in this city, and from that city all the nations of the world were to be blessed. Through the years, Jerusalem has caused great speculation. Just as in the days of the visit of the magi to Herod's palace, prophets and religious leaders have speculated concerning God's purposes in this city. Various theories have emerged concerning the place of Jerusalem in end time theology. Will a literal temple be built? Is the Church the new Israel? One thing I feel sure about is that God has a place in His plans for Jerusalem. I am also aware that in its destiny a 'new Jerusalem' is planned for the days ahead together with a *'new earth'* (Revelation 21:1).

The people

> *'Now the city was large and spacious, but there were few people in it, and the houses had not yet been rebuilt.'*   (Nehemiah 7:4)

In the story of salvation God has always looked for a people for Himself. Abraham set off towards an unknown destination simply trusting in the God that had called him. His trip was wrapped up in a search for a city whose architect and builder was

God (see Hebrews 11:10). The pilgrims who have walked the streets of Jerusalem were often looking for something beyond a physical city. Solomon, in building a magnificent temple, knew instinctively that a greater plan would unfold concerning a temple not made with human hands.

Just a list
Every generation of believers can play their part in the big picture of destiny. Ezra 2 and Nehemiah 7 consist of lists of exiles that returned to Jerusalem. In terms of daily devotions lists like these are not highly exciting, but in terms of destiny God saw it as important for these names to be included, for they represent stories of personal deliverance. Imagine having your name included in the Bible even though many readers through the ages may have skipped these sections. Not everyone made the Holy Scriptures, but even more are represented in a number listed under their clan head, for example, the descendants of Parosh 2,172 (Ezra 2:3), and the descendants of Delaiah, Tobiah and Nekoda 642 (Nehemiah 7:62). However, these are not just lists or numbers, but they represent a story of return, restoration and hope.

People and purpose
So God has always been looking for people. Firstly, there was the person Abraham and then there were the people of Israel. God loves to be with people. He calls people out from where they are, brings them out of exile and gathers them together. As the New Testament unfolds, the Church (*ekklesia*) emerges. God's purposes have moved from an individual to a nation, to a people called out of every nation, tribe and tongue.

A picture of a day to come
As I am writing, Baghdad has just been released from the grip of a dictator who has held people in bondage for thirty years. Vivid pictures of chains pulling down huge statues fill our newspapers. People are dancing in the streets. In the days of Ezra and Nehemiah, Babylon had held God's people captive. As they broke out of captivity and entered the city you can imagine the rejoicing that filled the air.

For believers there's a greater shout to come! In the future, city and people will once again be joined and at the heart of this story is a God who is longing to dwell with His people forever:

> *'I saw the Holy City, the new Jerusalem, coming down out of heaven from God, prepared as a bride beautifully dressed for her husband. And I heard a loud voice from the throne saying, "Now the dwelling of God is with men, and he will live with them."'*
>
> (Revelation 21:2–3)

God is looking for a people simply because He really wants to be with them. So hold your head high and join the list of those who are entering into God's promises.

PART 2

Transformation

Chapter 8

Transformation – the Transition

Having considered the issue of **rebuilding** we now move on to the area of **transformation**. It is my belief that this move is essential for the Church in Britain. As I have already stated, for a number of years we have concentrated on structure within our churches. Leaders have been encouraged to attend church growth seminars and attention has rightly been given to how the church organises itself. Whether it is through a 'cell model' or a 'programme model', much work has been focused on seeing God's people reshape in order to move on more effectively. However, the process needs to move on if our communities are to be changed for good. This requires a process of **transitioning**. Our emphasis increasingly needs to have an outward priority. The great commission must importantly remain as motivation. There is a world to reach and reshaping and re-emphasis must always be used for a purpose. Much attention has been placed upon the importance of each person within the Body of Christ and upon how each member fits alongside one another. Much teaching has centred on the need of discovering gifts, and we are now used to a church where counselling and care are more readily available. Though it has been essential for churches to grow in terms of maturity, the Church must now transition in terms of influence. Our reshaped churches need to breakout beyond our walls.

Transitioning takes time. As we begin to turn the Church 'outwards' we very soon discover that our thinking changes our attention and moves from the Christian community to the un-churched. We become more strategic in outward planning and our aim is in mobilising the Church to reach the lost. In his book, *Transitioning*,[1] Dan Southerland highlights three sets of leaders from the story of Nehemiah, under these headings:

1. **Secure the approval of the power brokers.**
   This involved the king, the queen, the governors, army officers and the cavalry.

2. **Secure the assistance of those whose help you will need.**
   This included governors of the surrounding lands and the keeper of the forest.

3. **Seek the advice of your vision team.**
   Nehemiah used hundreds to rebuild the wall but only a handful of choice men for his vision team.

In this helpful outline we move beyond the realm of God's community into the 'real world'. For Nehemiah, his focus was on the whole city of Jerusalem. One of our pastors at New Life in Lincoln, Mark Hutton, regularly prays for people of influence to join our fellowship. It is because he knows that it is important for us to become more relevant in our city and have a greater level of influence. Gradually, the church at New Life is thinking differently. Our world is becoming bigger. Another of our pastors, Alan Hoare, consistently encouraged us to invest in a large world map to display in the church building. He was so persistent that he eventually wore us down. I am pleased to say we are now confronted by the world every time we meet together, and our mission's work is promoted by the words 'Going Global'. In the last five years we have made large moves forward with regard to missions 'At home and away'.

I think it would be true to say that the emerging generation have a greater understanding of the need for the church to connect with community. Sometimes this has led to tensions, as these new, zealous believers do not always connect easily with the church as we have known it. They have often looked to reinvent church. This impetus is helping the church to move forward into its purpose but it is my belief that the generations need to work alongside each other to ensure that the 'gathered' aspect of the church is not lost. We need to learn from one another. Space for innovation and experimentation should be given, but it is my belief that relationships would be strengthened and communication increased. There is always the danger of fragmentation and if it is influence that we are looking for we are more likely to find it by being together than being apart. Yet another New Life Pastor, Malcolm Morgan, has historically worked closely with the youth, but is now moving his attention to the eighteen to thirties age group, seeking to inspire them to work in our city, but also to remain strongly connected within the church. Transition means movement and change. New challenges need to be faced.

In our own fellowship we have, for some time, been working on the following things in order to be more effective:

► *Vision and mission statements*

A sharper leadership structure. We now run with a 'Vision Core team' who are released by the wider leadership to keep the church moving forward.

► *Movement from maintenance to mission*

For the church this has meant more investment and emphasis to look outward.

► *Improved utilisation of our building*

Our building is now consistently used throughout the week. This involves groups such as 'mums and toddlers', creative art and educational classes in partnership with our local council. This means that over two hundred un-churched people cross our threshold each week.

► *Focused giving*

Far greater amounts of money are being released into mission's activity. This kind of giving is encouraged beyond people's tithes.

► *Releasing people's vision*

One example of this is our 'Creative Fellowship' initiative. From one of our lady's visions, hundreds of un-churched people have been on our arts courses. Art exhibitions have been welcomed by our local Public Library and a local Stationery and Art shop has opened its doors for our classes to take place on their premises.

► *Caring for the city*

Our intention is to release our members as 'salt and light' into our city; people who genuinely care and who are people of a 'different spirit', who in word and action live out their Christian faith.

In the transition there is much that we can do in terms of preparation. However, something beyond that needs to happen if we are to see transformation. This has to do with an element from above, something beyond our planning and human endeavour. It is that ingredient that only God can bring. It is possible for us to work on the 'form' but lack the power.

The second part of this book moves us beyond forms and structures into a heart-cry for greater change. There needs to be a transforming work of God that softens hearts, changes attitudes, breathes forgiveness and reconciliation, and heralds in a new era. In many ways, this goes beyond concepts of what we have called revival and moves towards fundamental changes within our society. The gospel we proclaim is a life-changing gospel. We are called to make a difference. In the chapter ahead we will see how in Ezra and Nehemiah the story moves beyond rebuilding into a transformed – though still not perfect – city. In the past church history there are many stories of this God dimension breaking in, of breathing on dying embers and bringing them back to life. Before you start reading Part 2 let me whet your appetite by quoting from an account of God moving in Argentina through the ministry of Tommy Hicks in *The Edge of Glory* by Dr Charles Carrin:

> 'In 1949 Tommy Hicks asked to meet Juan Perron, the dictator of Argentina. He wanted to request the use of the Atlantic Stadium for an evangelistic and healing crusade. Unable to get a meeting, Tommy Hicks prayed for a soldier on duty who was in great pain. He was immediately healed. This miracle opened the door to the President. "God opened a door for the gospel to invade the whole of South America." That young soldier's healing was only the first of a long list of miraculous works the Holy Spirit would do. [As I read these words I thought of how God opened the door for Nehemiah.] The President was seriously distressed by severe eczema that covered his body. Tommy Hicks prayed and the eczema left his body. "With everyone in the room looking on, Juan Perron's skin suddenly became as soft and clear as a baby's. 'Dios, mio! Estoy sanado!' Perron exclaimed. 'My

God! I am healed!' and he was."' As you can imagine having use of the stadium was no longer a problem, and great crowds began to attend.'

Dr Carrin continues:

'The Holy Spirit fell in power, and thousands upon thousands were healed. Many thousands more were saved as God began revival in Argentina that has no parallel in modern times. He turned Argentina upside down and planted the tree of the gospel deeply in the soil. God's hand was "stretched out over all the nations" (Isaiah 14:26); there was no turning back.'[2]

This amazing move of the Spirit has been revitalised over the past ten years as fresh outpourings have been experienced. The Church has been strengthened and many have been brought into the Kingdom. However, the recent financial collapse in Argentina challenges me with some questions. Have the years of revival failed to impact the decision makers in the nation? Has government been impacted? Has society been changed?

Revival in the church needs to move on into transformation within our society:

'We need to see the equivalent of the Lord Shaftebury's and William Wilberforce's emerge in making a long lasting change in our nation again.'[3]

Notes

1. Dan Southerland, *Transitioning* (Zondervan, 2002)
2. Charles Carrin, *The Edge of Glory* (Creation House Press, 2001).
3. Dan Southerland, *Transitioning* (Zondervan, 2002).

Chapter 9

Transformation – the Devotion

Ezra and Nehemiah point us to a season of strong devotion and commitment. All the evidence, with regard to stories of transformation today, highlights high levels of devotion. In this chapter we will see that devotion is the backdrop to the unfolding picture.

When news of the downfall of Jerusalem hits the ears of Nehemiah he instinctively moves into a season of prayer and fasting. There is much that we can learn from the opening pages of Nehemiah with regard to his intense devotion. Personally, when bad news comes to me I have a tendency to take a dive. Were you to ask Irene, she would tell you that one problem brought to me on a Monday morning can quickly grow in size, until by lunch I assume that everything will fall apart. I have much to learn. Nehemiah's response started with 'weeping' but quickly moved into fasting and prayer.

The results of devotion

A new kind of praying

The following outline shows the breadth of prayer life and the maturity of the man. It reveals prayer levels that are a challenge to today's Church. Our prayer meetings need something of this passion and focus if transformation is to take place.

His prayer begins with reverence and adoration:

> 'O LORD, God of heaven, the great and awesome God, who keeps his covenant of love with those who love him and obey his commands.' (Nehemiah 1:5)

In these few words we become aware of the high regard in which
God is held. He has a vision of the greatness of God. If there is
to be breakthrough then it will be God that will bring it. This
new kind of praying involves persistence and perseverance, as
Nehemiah brings his requests *'day and night'* (Nehemiah 1:6)
before the Lord. It also involves confession and identification:

> *'I confess the sins we Israelites, including myself and my father's
> house, have committed against you.'*   (Nehemiah 1:6)

Nehemiah is not just praying for a situation; he wraps himself up
in the God-given burden. He acknowledges his own sins. How
refreshing for a leader to say 'including myself'. It is this kind of
open prayer that gets heaven's attention. From confession he
then moves on to supplication. He reminds God of the promises
He has made, promises of blessing and gathering, if the people
humbly return in repentance. His prayers are filled with passion
and emotion but ultimately become very specific and focused:

> *'Give your servant success today by granting him favour in the
> presence of this man.'*   (Nehemiah 1:11)

He targets the great King Artaxerxes and expects results. It is not
long before 'this man' becomes part of an answered prayer.

A new paradigm

When Ezra becomes aware of the depth of sin in the nation, he
responds in a way that is unfamiliar to the British mindset. Put it
down to his Jewish temperament if you want, but this man of
God becomes animated and disturbed:

> *'When I heard this, I tore my tunic and cloak, pulled hair from my
> head and beard and sat down appalled.'*   (Ezra 9:3)

Please don't misunderstand me. I'm not suggesting that all
intercessors should de-robe and de-hair, but you couldn't accuse
this man of complacency! Surely it's time that we 'felt' something and become passionate about what we believe. Ezra was
not deranged or prone to tantrums, but he held two things in
tension. He saw God's laws broken and abandoned, yet caught a
glimpse of a new society and new order that could be fought for:

> *'Then, at the evening sacrifice, I rose from my self-abasement,*
> *with my tunic and cloak torn, and fell on my knees with my*
> *hands spread out to the LORD my God and prayed.'* (Ezra 9:5)

This kind of praying is contagious. I am grateful to God that today He is raising up a new band of young people and students who are pushing out the boundaries of prayer, as we have known it. 24–7 initiatives are leading the way for passion and prayer to connect again.

> *'While Ezra was praying and confessing, weeping and throwing*
> *himself down before the house of God, a large crowd of Israelites –*
> *men, women and children – gathered around him. They too wept*
> *bitterly.'* (Ezra 10:1)

This praying received attention and changes began to take place.

A new kind of celebrating

So far we have looked at devotion from a personal perspective, but something corporate also begins to emerge. Certain times in the Old Testament were given over to seasons of great celebration. It is interesting that, during the rebuilding days of Ezra and Nehemiah, the people begin to celebrate again. In Chapter 1 we looked at a shift in Britain with regard to worship. Today large celebrations for worship are commonplace. Some would argue that the church is 'celebrated out'. I would argue that we have only just begun. Why are days of celebration so important?

- We can declare the high praise of God.
- We can join hearts and souls in unison with thousands of other believers.
- We can set aside all distractions and work for a period of time.
- We can enjoy the best in terms of musicianship and creativity.
- We can release children into a similar dynamic.
- We can create a platform and throne for Jesus to be glorified.

The dictionary defines 'celebration' in the following ways: 'to commemorate joyfully – to make famous as by song or poem –

to observe with solemn rites'. When studying celebrations and festivals in the Scriptures, I found that these were very special days that marked out important occasions.

Foundation days

Celebration took place when the foundations of the new temple were laid. Ezra 3:10–12 describes the excitement as the builders laid the foundations. This involved high levels of worship, praise and thanksgiving, concluding with the words, *'and all the people gave a great shout of praise to the* LORD, *because the foundation of the house of the* LORD *was laid'* (Ezra 3:11). This was not a pleasant ceremony with little speeches and greetings, or the presenting of a silver trowel; this was full-blown celebration, so much so that *'the sound was heard far away'* (Ezra 3:13).

Dedication days

Further celebrating took place when the building work was completed. As the temple was set apart and consecrated for the Lord's work, the people were again led in celebration:

> *'Then the people of Israel ... celebrated the dedication of the house of God with joy.'*   (Ezra 6:16)

Also, as the walls are brought back to their former glory, huge attention was given to a pageant of choirs, marches, music and sounds of rejoicing. Check out the festivities in Nehemiah 12.

Renewal days

A similar picture can be found in the days of Hezekiah when the service of the temple of the Lord was re-established (see 2 Chronicles 29:35–36). During these days of renewal we find sacrifice, singing, bowing, kneeling and glad worship. In fact, during Passover in these seasons of renewal, the word 'celebrate' or 'celebration' occurs eight times. I believe that this kind of celebrating carries with it a sound that attracts heaven.

Celebrating the Word

For some who may feel that the emphasis in this chapter has been too much towards experience and emotion, I conclude these thoughts on 'devotion' with an emphasis brought in Nehemiah 8:

'All the people assembled as one man in the square before the Water Gate. They told Ezra the scribe to bring out the Book of the Law of Moses, which the Lord had commanded for Israel.'
(Nehemiah 8:1)

The Word was read aloud and celebrated. In my early years of church planting, on reading this passage, we decided to give space in our church programme each week for the public reading of the Word. On these occasions we had no commentary or discussion but simply listened to the Bible being read. It became a great discipline for what turned out to be a very fruitful season.

We read that, *'all the people listened attentively'* (Nehemiah 8:3). It was at this time that the first church pulpit was put in place, in order that all could hear and see. As the book was read, the people worshipped.

We look today for a re-emergence of the Spirit and the Word. We also look for people to not only listen to the Word but to be changed by the Word. Again, the people in our story *'celebrate with great joy, because they now understood the words that had been made known to them'* (Nehemiah 8:12).

May new levels of prayer, passion, worship and the Word, position us for the transformation of our communities in our time.

Chapter 10

Transformation – the Culture

It is one thing to affect structures, but it is another to affect attitudes, behaviour and culture. It is relatively easy these days to change a church meeting night, but much more difficult to change the heart of those who meet. The challenge is to see a church 'beyond the meeting'; a church impacting and affecting society and a church with a different spirit. It was reported of Caleb and Joshua that they were men of a different spirit (see Numbers 14:24). This meant that they didn't follow the crowd, had a positive confession and followed after the Lord whole-heartedly. Rather than being shaped by what was around them, they chose to sow a different spirit. It is this kind of thinking that will transform communities.

The revival in Argentina has been an inspiration to believers across the world. Thousands have been impacted and stories are told of churches being open day and night for worship services. Many have been swept into the Kingdom and the effects of this work of God have been wonderful. However, Argentina as a nation has faced incredible social upheaval and financial challenges. It is no doubt that through the prayer of the church what has happened in the spiritual life of Argentina will push through to affect the very heart of the whole nation.

In the days of Ezra and Nehemiah, social changes became a part of the restoration process as the city of Jerusalem was impacted. From this city, the whole of the nation would be affected for good. In Nehemiah 5, the emphasis moves away from the structures of walls and gates towards the issues of community life. The simple truth is that for transformation to take place it must impact the poor. Nehemiah begins to speak into the issues of inequality and injustice that had pervaded the people. Many had become ensnared with financial pressures. Interest levels were high and extortion and corruption had invaded society. Nehemiah called for change and demanded that those that had been on the make should repay money and give back property and land. Restoration meant that restitution should be made.

For the gospel to impact our cities it must carry with it a burden to see injustice addressed and the poor helped. Not only should the Word be taught but also the poor should be fed. After Ezra's reading of the Word, things began to change. The Israelites began to confess their sins.

Results of culture change

Days of community change
Nehemiah 9 recounts how days began to have a different meaning. Priorities changed and the Bible says that a quarter of the day was given to the reading of the Word and another quarter to confession and worship. For many Christians an hour on a Sunday is too much to ask for, but here were people who were dedicating their days to change. This led them into changed attitudes and eventually to a binding agreement:

> *'In view of all this, we are making a binding agreement, putting it in writing, and our leaders, our Levites and our priests are affixing their seals to it.'* (Nehemiah 9:38)

This was not an emotional response to an appeal at the end of a meeting, this was a decision to live differently and clean up their behaviour. They were now determined to make a difference by being different.

Rediscovering a New Testament church culture
Some time ago Francois van Niekerk, from Pretoria, South Africa, was invited to speak at one of our leadership forums. Instead of launching into the expected talk, he held up two pictures painted by an artist in his church. The first was a picture of a plantation with trees in neat rows and the second was of a forest. This second picture was composed of trees and bushes of

different sizes and colours and had a natural, or even 'untidy' appearance. Francois then asked the gathered leaders what type of church we were looking to build. For many of us, the thought of a neat and tidy church with everything well ordered seemed appealing, but our attention was drawn to the forest, or 'God's garden', where the trees and bushes differing in size and colour were allowed to grow. This encapsulated for me something that I have believed for many years; that Our Father is the gardener and what He grows, I want to be a part of. This took me back to scriptures that had led me into New Testament church structures and on re-reading my eyes began to see what I am calling 'New Testament church culture'. I became interested in the 'soil' in which plants and trees grow.

There is often pressure, particularly upon church leaders, to make things happen. In wanting the best, many of us have sought to learn from various moves of the Spirit throughout the world. This has been healthy and good, but has led to a tendency to try to import that special ingredient that will bring us the long-awaited breakthrough. Leaders have visited Toronto, Pensacola, Argentina, Brazil or Singapore to find the missing ingredient. Most who have visited these places have benefited from the experience and been blessed, but most have also realised that to bring back a new structure without connecting with the culture or life of that place can bring a sense of disillusionment, or even failure. On recognising this, I revisited Bible passages that had led me in my early years of ministry. When looking again at one passage in particular, it was as though I was reading the verses through different eyes. Excited by what I thought I was seeing, I telephoned my friend in America, Jack Groblewski, to talk through my findings. We talked together about New Testament church culture and, during our conversation, I asked him for a definition of the word 'culture'. Without a great deal of thought he gave me the following definition, which I include partly to illustrate what I am about to share, but also because I was so impressed that Jack could give such a definition so quickly. He said, 'Culture is the consensus of values, morals, customs and manners which are reached by a collection of people.'

In the early New Testament church there was a way of doing things; a 'soil' in which the church was growing, a kind of DNA that held it together. I wanted to try to rediscover this New Testament culture, so that structures could follow life, rather than the other way round. On reading extracts from Tommy Tenney's book *God's Favorite House* this discovery seemed to be underlined. He writes, 'Structures will follow passion just as marriage follows love.'[1] I had thought of 'structures' for years; now I was on a quest to find the 'life'.

The passage I turned to was Acts 2:42–47. In my early years of ministry I had often been to this passage of Scripture to see how church should be. What kind of meetings did the early Christians attend? Where did they meet? And so on. From these guidelines we had learned the importance of good Bible teaching, of fellowship, communion and prayer. Years ago we had also looked at 'community'. In fact, a close friend of mine left us to join a 'Christian community' believing that our kind of church was too worldly. We often looked at these verses in terms of structure, programmes and meetings. All of these things, of course, were valid and instructive but on re-visiting this passage I found myself looking a little deeper and this is what I found:

▶   *A culture of devotion* (Acts 2:42)

Though, of course, apostles' teaching, fellowship, breaking of bread and prayer were essential, the word that stood out for me was the word 'devoted'. It was this word that caused the above to flourish. In today's world, people tend to shy away from commitment, or at the very least put a timeframe on it. These early believers were not forced to be 'devoted'. There was no three-line whip to be at the prayer meeting; they just simply wanted to belong. They had met Jesus and that was enough.

I have fond memories of a group of young people who lived in this 'devotion' culture. At one particular meeting, I was issued with a challenge: 'We will give you our school half-term holiday if you will teach us what you know.' I responded to this challenge but soon realised that five long days would be hard to fill. In fact, by Tuesday I had run out of prepared material and had to rely on God for the rest of the week, to help me through. Of course I made out that I was well prepared, but in truth I had never worked this way before. The beauty of this story is that, out of that group, one now leads worship, another is a care worker attached to our church, and a third runs our Alpha courses. Plants that flourish are those that grow in the soil of commitment and devotion.

► **A culture of faith** (Acts 2:43)

It's a pressure to perform miracles. Perhaps creating a culture of expectation and faith is the starting point. David Wang, a wonderful man from Hong Kong who has witnessed many miracles, also supports Manchester United! Whilst he was sharing in our church he banged his chest and said, 'My heart beats faith.' This was a man who was at rest in the knowledge that God is the miracle worker. Our responsibility is to fill our lungs with the air of faith. Sometimes our upbringing and education makes this difficult.

► **A culture of unity** (Acts 2:44 and 46)

For many years this concept has been an inspiration to me. I have longed to see believers walking together and churches joining together for the purpose of transforming communities. However, there is a tendency to think structurally, and we try to find the lowest common denominator for meeting. We have also learned the importance of cell groups from these verses but have discovered that it is possible to have united meetings with no unity and cell groups without meaningful relationship. When a church has discovered a culture of unity, it will be easier to structure later.

► **A culture of generosity** (Acts 2:45)

When reading this verse literally, many have thought that to please God they would have to sell everything and join a Christian community. Though by doing this I am sure many have found blessing, I believe that something simpler is at the heart of this verse. I have become wary of systems that pressurise believers into things that condemn or burden. Jesus came to lift burdens, not to give us more. What was happening in the early Church was voluntary and natural. The life of God within them produced a generosity that wanted to see others blessed. I don't believe this is a blueprint for deserting the world and finding a holy and protected utopia. I believe heaven can be found 'on earth' and in the darkest of places.

► **A culture of growth** (Acts 2:47)

How do churches grow? There are church growth seminars that will help and principles to follow, but how liberating to know that, ultimately, it is God who makes things grow. This doesn't mean we just sit back and watch as we were designed to be co-workers with Christ, but something intriguing was happening in the early Church. It had a growth gene. It couldn't help it – it had to grow! This is the culture we need to rediscover. The church in Britain is intended to grow. Perhaps, in one sense, it is time to relax, stop striving and enjoy the life that God has given us. These early believers *'ate together with glad and sincere hearts ... enjoying the favour of all the people'* (Acts 2:46–47). I have a strong feeling that attitudes will determine the culture in which we grow.

Chuck Swindoll says:

'The longer I live, the more I realise the impact of attitude on life. Attitude, to me, is more important than facts. It is more important than the past, than education, than money, than circumstances, than failures, than successes, than what other people think or say or do. It is more important than appearance, giftedness or skill. It will make or break a company, a church, a home. The remarkable thing is that we have a choice every day regarding the attitude we will embrace for that day. We cannot change our past; we cannot change the fact that people will act in a certain way. We cannot change the inevitable. The only thing we can do is to play on the one string we have, and that is our attitude. I am convinced that life is 10% what happens to me and 90% how I react to it. And so it is with you, we are in charge of our attitudes.'[2]

Maybe a different people, walking a different way with a different attitude can make a difference.

This section from the *Natural Church Development Handbook* by Christian A. Schwartz[3] illustrates for me that 'culture' is important in these eight quality characteristics of growing churches:

1. **Empowering** leadership
2. **Gift-orientated** ministry
3. **Passionate** spirituality
4. **Functional** structures
5. **Inspiring** worship services

6.   **Holistic** small groups
7.   **Need-orientated** evangelism
8.   **Loving** relationships

All of the above are to be found in growing churches of many different kinds all over the world. These churches (trees) may well be very different but they are growing in very special soil that I would describe as a 'New Testament church culture.'

Notes
1. Tommy Tenney, *God's Favourite House* (Destiny Image, 1999).
2. Chuck Swindoll quoted by John Maxwell in *Developing the Leader Within You* (Thomas Nelson, 2000).
3. Christian A. Schwartz, *Natural Church Development Handbook* (British Church Growth Association, 2002).

Chapter 11

Transformation – the Focus

It was essential that Nehemiah had set his *'face like flint'* (Isaiah 50:7). There were many possible distractions and so often circumstances seemed to be against him. Keeping focused is perhaps one of the biggest challenges for church leaders today. There are so many options and possibilities. Dale Gentry, a prophet from America, spoke very accurately some years ago into our situation. I can still hear his words ringing in my ears; 'Voices, voices, I hear many voices.' Dale was hearing that in our church, at that time, there were many opinions and we needed to concentrate on hearing the voice of God. Since then we have worked hard on clearly formulating the primary thing God is calling us to. Jesus set His face toward Jerusalem. Paul declared, *'One thing I do'* (Philippians 3:13), and church leaders need to hear the voice of God. Three words have been important to me in this quest:

▶ *Direction*

It is vital that we keep moving forward. The dictionary defines 'direction' as 'the position of one point in relation to another without reference to the intervening distance'. This will require leaders to look to the future and take a hold of it.

▶ *Concentration*

Again the dictionary definition is, 'to draw to a common centre'. This involves setting our sight on the most important thing. I can so easily lose my concentration and too readily find compromise creeping up on me.

▶ **Delegation**

We need to learn to pass on that which is non-essential. This should not be abdication but as D.L. Moody said, 'I would rather set ten men to work than do the work of ten men.'[1]

The key verse regarding focus is found in Nehemiah 6

> *'I am carrying on a great project and cannot go down.'*
>
> (Nehemiah 6:3)

There was much happening, as we shall see, to seek to pull Nehemiah from his task. There were many voices calling him down, but with dogged determination he kept on going. At this point we would do well to settle the fact in our minds that if we want to do any meaningful thing for God, there will be opposition. In his excellent book *Transitioning,'*[2] Dan Southerland highlights five different kinds of opposition from the book of Nehemiah:

1. Expect apathy
2. Expect anger
3. Expect ridicule
4. Expect criticism
5. Expect a fight

We have already looked, in some detail, at the opposition Nehemiah encountered, but it is worth reminding ourselves also of the reality of the battle we are in. The people needed to carry swords and trowels. We certainly need to be wary when all men speak well of us. Dan Southerland also wrote, 'the reality is that criticism and opposition will drive you somewhere. Let it drive you closer to God and you will become better; let it drive you away from God and you will become bitter.'[3]

Results of loss of focus

Diversion

Sanballat and Geshem tried to lure Nehemiah down from the walls. Having lost in the head-on approach, they now moved to the gentle method of negotiation and politicking:

> *'Come, let us meet together in one of the villages on the plain of Ono.'*   (Nehemiah 6:2)

They schemed to meet him in a 'neutral' venue in order to negotiate. In real terms this was a diversion. For leaders, it is so easy to be drawn by other people's agendas that on the surface may look attractive. Even in the simple day-to-day issues of church life we need to be careful that the many good ideas out there are not, in reality, distractions.

Subversion
It is essential that we surround ourselves with under-liners rather than under-miners. There are too many Sanballats or Absaloms who are looking to subvert. They undermine authority figures and tap away, like woodpeckers, at trust.

Abortion
The enemy is out to kill, steal and destroy. He targets embryo vision and drains the life from projects before their completion. He erodes people's self-worth, ridicules their integrity, and wants to spit them out in disgrace. Not only have projects been destroyed but good men and women have been wounded and hurt in the process.

Requirements of focus

A call for bravery
Transitioning a church from maintenance to mission is not an easy process. Even friends are likely to say, 'You're not as interested in me as you used to be.' Congregation members may accuse you of no longer being a good shepherd to them. Other ministers may question your motives but if, with sensitivity, you pursue what God is calling you to, you will complete the wall. Once the wall is up don't expect too much recognition. Often leadership is only noticed when there is a problem or crisis. Take heart and be brave. God's work is more important than our reputations. It is what God thinks about us that is the most important thing. Also, bear in mind that when one project is finished, there will be others to take on. Vision remains a journey and once, by faith, we have left the ground, we need more faith to keep us flying.

Leadership, leadership, leadership

Having read through Ezra and Nehemiah I cannot escape the issue of leadership. God seems to choose and work through people. Phil Vogel in *Making Apprentices* writes, 'The future of the church will be determined by the quality of its leadership.'[4] The Church today needs a particular kind of leader. The Scriptures give us guidelines and qualifications to look for in leaders, but in today's pressured and fragmented world a new breed of men and women need to emerge who know how to focus. It is a joy to see people emerging who, at a young age, seem to possess the kind of ingredients necessary for today's church. I have mentioned the Dream Centre in Los Angeles. Closer to home, I am privileged to be advising Dave Smith, a young man, who has a heart to see a large strategic church emerge in Peterborough. Plans are being drawn for an impressive facility that will give substance to his vision. I only regret that, when I was younger, I did not see then what I see today. Ladies like Heidi Baker, who are pioneering great things for God, inspire me. She, together with her husband Rolland, has planted many churches in Mozambique. Paul's words to the church in Corinth remain a challenge:

> 'Even though you have ten thousand guardians in Christ, you do not have many fathers.'　　　　　　(1 Corinthians 4:15)

Mentoring and parenting is still a scarce commodity but more leaders with a heart after God need to connect with those who have gone before. I believe they will then go further than we have managed to go and do more than we have managed to do. I believe these new leaders will need the following:

- Passionate love for Jesus
- Team players
- Servant hearts
- Loyalty
- To be teachable
- Willingness to be accountable
- Ability to see the bigger picture
- Flexibility
- A non-denominational attitude

- To be biblical
- Openness to the Holy Spirit
- Ablity to focus

It may well be that there are many in God's preparation school who are waiting to emerge.

Notes
1. Quoted by Andrew Le Peau in *Paths of Leadership* (Scripture Union, 1984).
2. Dan Southerland, *Transitioning* (Zondervan, 2002).
3. *Ibid.*
4. Philip Vogel, *Go and Make Apprentices* (Kingsway Publications, 1986).

Chapter 12

Transformation – the Lifestyle

As Ezra read from the Book of the Law in front of the Water Gate, *'the people listened attentively'*(Nehemiah 8:3). Their response was one of worship and praise, mixed with tears and weeping. What followed was just like Christmas celebrations as the people ate and drank and gave out presents. New understanding brought a new release. This was not just an emotional response to good news from God's Word; there was a new recognition that obedience was required. This led to the reinstatement of festivals that had been lost for years and the corporate confession of sin.

> *'On the twenty-fourth day of the same month, the Israelites gathered together, fasting and wearing sackcloth and having dust on their heads.'* (Nehemiah 9:1)

Requirements of transformed lifestyle

Never forget to remember

During this time Levites began to address the people. After encouraging the people to praise the Lord they then began to recount the history of the people of God. Beginning with Abram, they took the listeners through the stories of God's dealings with them and particularly pointed out God's plan of deliverance and salvation. Great emphasis was laid upon God's faithfulness and His heart to set people free.

Everyone was encouraged to remember the great acts of deliverance in his or her history. The following outline of Nehemiah 9 shows the emphasis the Levites brought in order to arrest the people's attention.

- The covenant with Abraham (Nehemiah 9:8)
- The deliverance from Egypt (Nehemiah 9:9)
- The divided Red Sea (Nehemiah 9:10)
- The guidance of cloud and fire (Nehemiah 9:12)
- The Law at Sinai (Nehemiah 9:13)
- The provision of bread from heaven (Nehemiah 9:15)
- The guidance in the desert (Nehemiah 9:19)
- The sustaining power of God in the desert (Nehemiah 9:21)
- The possession of the Promised Land (Nehemiah 9:22)
- The promised blessings of fruitfulness and growth (Nehemiah 9:23)
- The victories in battle (Nehemiah 9:24)
- The patience of God (Nehemiah 9:30)
- The warnings of prophets (Nehemiah 9:31)

Over and again, this brief history is interrupted by descriptions of God's faithfulness and His character. God is described as *'a forgiving God, gracious and compassionate, slow to anger and abounding in love'* (Nehemiah 9:17). It also says in that God shows *'great compassion'* (Nehemiah 9:19), and we see the *'good Spirit'* (Nehemiah 9:20) instructs them.

> *'From heaven you heard them, and in your great compassion you gave them deliverers.'* (Nehemiah 9:27)

God is seen as unchanging and merciful:

> *'But in your great mercy you did not put an end to them or abandon them, for you are a gracious and merciful God.'* (Nehemiah 9:31)

God is a God who keeps His promises. He is mighty and awesome and above all, He is a God who stands by His covenant of love, who acts justly on every page of unfolding history.

Remember the bad

I am aware that in my life there is a tendency to forget the bad.
Irene has to remind me often that my remembrance of the 'good
old days' has not always been quite accurate. Sometimes, the
sands of time have covered some painful memories, but it still
remains important that we remember the bad and that in this
remembering, we keep a perspective for the future. As the Levites
recount God's faithfulness in the episodes of history, they also
highlight the mistakes and shortcomings of God's unfaithful
people. Again a study of this chapter shows the many times
God's people fail to obey. The Levites make sure they remember
the bad, and some of the illustrations are as follows:

> *'But they, our forefathers, became arrogant and stiff-necked, and
> did not obey your commands.'*   (Nehemiah 9:16)

> *'They refused to listen.'*   (Nehemiah 9:17)

> *'But they were disobedient and rebelled against you; they put your
> law behind their backs.'*   (Nehemiah 9:26)

> *'But as soon as they were at rest, they again did what was evil in
> your sight.'*   (Nehemiah 9:28)

> *'Stubbornly they turned their backs on you, became stiff-necked
> and refused to listen.'*   (Nehemiah 9:29)

Two key requirements for 'lifestyle change'

Two pictures become very clear for me in Nehemiah 9 that, if
seen and embraced, set the scene for a change of attitude and
heart that will lead to change in lifestyle.

1. Remember the faithfulness of a covenant-keeping God.
2. Remember and acknowledge the sinfulness, disobedience
   and stiff-necked nature of God's people.

Acknowledging where we are at and 'coming clean' are essential
if we are to move forward. The concluding verse of the chapter
shows how the people agree with God's Word and pledge to start
again:

'In view of all this, we are making a binding agreement, putting it in writing, and our leaders, our Levites and our priests are affixing their seals to it.'   (Nehemiah 9:38)

Notice the interesting choice of words used; the leaders have become 'our' leaders, the Levites 'our' Levites, and the priests 'our' priests. When things are put right with God, we somehow begin to embrace and love one another. I have noticed that when people are 'out of sorts' with the church it is often, 'your' church and 'your' leaders. Once people take responsibility we are all in it together.

▶ **Things begin to change**

Transformation is about change. Teaching is only effective if it results in change. The Levites faithfully delivered the Word, but would the people change, and if they did change would the change be permanent?

▶ **They sealed the agreement**

The people knew their fickle history and as a result, put their names to the agreement. This made them accountable. When we put our names to things it has to count. They were willing to be numbered and noticed.

▶ **They separated themselves**

Following years of compromise the people separated themselves from the nations around them. They re-committed themselves to the Law of God. This meant purifying relationships, keeping the Sabbath, and honouring those things that are holy.

▶ **They served the House of God**

'We assume the responsibility for carrying out the commands to give a third of a shekel each year for the service of the House of our God.'   (Nehemiah 10:32)

The people brought the first of their crops, grain, fruit and oil and began to tithe again. As lifestyles begin to be transformed, God's house becomes more and more important. With new levels of unity they declare: *'We will not neglect the house of our God'* (Nehemiah 10:39).

▶ **They settled in Jerusalem**

As Nehemiah 11 opens, so a new chapter opened for Jerusalem. This city that had lain in ruins now began to live again. The new people were being prepared for the newly rebuilt city. Lists were prepared of the returning families, the gatekeepers, priests and Levites.

▶ **They secured their future**

In Nehemiah 13, Nehemiah moved into his 'final reforms'. It was essential that any changes were not just cosmetic. Things done at this point of time would have a long-reaching effect into the days ahead. What was needed was *'fruit that will last'* (John 15:16). In this final chapter of Nehemiah the desire to 'clean the house' is followed through with persistence and zeal. The requirements of the Law had to be met. Ammonites and Moabites were removed from the assembly as required by the law. Though this seems harsh in today's understanding, this should be seen as a desire for sanctification. There had been years of compromise, self-seeking and hidden agendas.

Tobiah, one of the early aggressors against God's plans, had even manipulated his way into the temple courts. Eliashib, the High Priest, had allowed him *'a room in the courts of the house of God'* (Nehemiah 13:7). Can you imagine giving the enemy this foothold? If this threat were not removed, a new cycle of enemy activity would have ultimately emerged. Nehemiah wanted to secure a period of peace for the days ahead. With boldness, Nehemiah dealt with the problem. He says:

> *'I was greatly displeased and threw all Tobiah's household goods out of the room. I gave orders to purify the rooms, and I then put back into them the equipment of the house of God, with the grain offerings and the incense.'* (Nehemiah 13:8–9)

I am tempted to digress at this point and think about the many footholds that the enemy has acquired within the Church. For fear of being misunderstood, many things are left un-addressed. In some churches it is difficult to walk on the carpet because of all the issues that have been swept under it. All I would say is that it would be wise to remove Tobiah from the minister's vestry.

Nehemiah then begins to address issues of inequality and

neglect. The Levites had not been adequately taken care of. This led to a rebuke: *'Why is the house of God neglected?'* (Nehemiah 13:11). I believe that today God's house is increasingly lower down the list of people's priorities. Recently, these scriptures have pointed me, in my own life, to be deeply grateful for the Church of Jesus Christ. I count it an honour to be included in His Body. Christians are a privileged people. Nehemiah had realised that God's people had become lax. The Sabbath was no longer a special day given to the Lord, and the Jewish heritage had become blurred by compromise and neglect. Today, with our New Testament understanding, we don't have to look to follow rules and regulations, and we should, I believe, take a firm hold of the principles that Nehemiah brought us. We need to be wholehearted in our faith, and to seek first the Kingdom of God.

Watch your language

As every area of communal life is looked at, Nehemiah realises that 'mixture' has invaded God's people. God had given strict orders on the dangers of being joined to people outside of the covenant promises. Such was the compromise that:

> *'Half of their children spoke the language of Ashdod, or the language of one of the other peoples, and did not know how to speak the language of Judah.'*   (Nehemiah 13:24)

What an amazing verse. The descendants of Abraham no longer spoke his language nor did they know his God.

Pastoral sensitivity

Enough was enough. Nehemiah was so angry that he said it as he felt it. The following should not appear in manuals for pastoral ministry:

> *'I rebuked them and called curses down on them. I beat some of the men and pulled out their hair. I made them take an oath in God's name and said: "You are not to give your daughters in marriage to their sons, nor are you to take their daughters in marriage for your sons or for yourselves."'*   (Nehemiah 13:25)

I think this could be termed 'heavy shepherding!' However, it cannot be denied that he passionately wanted the best for the days ahead.

Following further cleansing procedures – not unlike Jesus' response years later in the temple – the scene was set for a new beginning. His final words were, *'Remember me with favour, O my God'* (Nehemiah 13:31).

Chapter 13

Transformation – the Stories

If you are like me, you want to know whether the stories of transformation that hit the media are for real. It is relatively easy to put a spin on revival stories that make them seem more impressive than they really are. However, the following stories are not only credible for me because they appear in books and videos, but also because of the knowledge I have received either through personal contacts, or from the testimonies of close friends. The following three stories highlight the power of transformation. It is these kind of stories that encourage us with the possibilities of communities being changed by the gospel. These are testimonies of a church that moves beyond personal devotion and begins to affect the society around.

Story 1 – Kiambu, Kenya

This amazing story is captured on the *Transformations 1* video, hosted by George Otis Jr.[1] I also spent some time with my good friend and fellow 'bridge-crosser', Duane White, from Texas. Duane has so far made five trips to Kiambu and has ministered into the church in Kenya for several years. Ten years ago, Kiambu had a bad reputation, so much so that in the late 1980s it had one of the highest crime rates in Kenya. This town of sixty-five thousand people was a notorious 'ministry graveyard'. There were no effective evangelical churches. It was into this problem area that Thomas and Margaret Muchee and their two children received a call from God. They soon began asking God to show them the source of the oppression on the community. They identified a spirit of witchcraft that was gripping the lives of the people. One particular evil door being opened was through 'Mama Jane', a woman purporting to be a Christian, but who

97

was actually involved in witchcraft. After an extensive period of prayer and fasting, Thomas embarked on an outdoor crusade. In the first week two hundred people came to Christ. The battle was on as an enemy counter-attack brought despondency onto God's people. The church elders took authority, fasted and prayed, and 'Mama Jane' packed up and left town.

During October and November 2000, Duane White visited Kiambu taking along a friend. On his return to America the friend became seriously ill, and within hours was close to death. In a vision Duane saw a picture of a witchdoctor putting a curse on him. Following a time of prayer and fasting, the curse was broken and he made a full recovery. Duane witnessed firsthand the impact of this on the community. In the hotel where he stayed he asked questions about the changes. Everyone he spoke to talked of the amazing turnaround in Kiambu, even though they were not all aware of the presence of the Christian church. In the last ten years the change has been dramatic. Now Kiambu has one of the lowest crime rates, and the population has increased by 30% because it is now a desirable place to live.

The main church – Word of Faith – led by Thomas, is now three to four thousand strong and two hundred other churches have been planted. They continue to plant outwards and also have a desire to reach the Sudan. What then has been the secret? Clearly prayer and fasting have been major keys in the break-through. The church was soon nicknamed 'The Prayer Cave' and often up to two hundred believers a day are found praying and fasting. Under the new auditorium they are building many 'prayer stalls' with just enough room for a person to lie down. People simply collect a mat and go to prayer.

I asked Duane what he felt were the key things that had taken place. He mentioned the following:

▶ *Economic transformation*

There has been no doubt that as the gospel has been preached there has been a 'lift factor'. People now want to move into the area and the economy has experienced an upturn.

▶ *Social reform*

Again, due to the proclamation of the gospel, the social order of things has changed. Crime rates have dramatically come down, bars have closed and alcoholism reduced.

► **Entrepreneurial changes**

As businesses have begun to flourish a number of believers have creatively got involved. The church administration bought a local bar and turned it into *Mt. Hebron Café*. Its main ministry now is to feed the street children.

There is no doubt in my mind that Kiambu has experienced a community transformation.

Story 2 – Almalonga, Guatemala

Once again this story appears on the *Transformations 1* video, but I have also included anecdotal material from my good friends in Norway, Trygve and Barbro Brekke. Having watched the video Trygve and Barbro wanted to see things firsthand. Almalonga is a town of approximately twenty thousand people. Twenty years ago it was a community in total poverty. Alcoholism, idolatry and witchcraft were widespread. It is now clean and prosperous and is a 'city of churches' with eight out of ten people considering themselves to be Christians. So what has taken place? Before the transformation Almalonga was a dangerous place to visit. Drunken men would literally lie on the streets and the four jails were often so full that some criminals had to be transferred to other places. Not only was alcohol a major problem, but also many people had made pacts with folk idols that exerted power over their lives. Any visiting evangelists were usually chased away. The small community of believers began to fast and pray, very often for three or four days a week. As they prayed the churches began to grow. God began to show Himself strongly, and signs and wonders began to happen. Teresa, a local believer, was taken to church in a very serious condition. Her internal organs had begun to rot, and the smell of death was on her. Friends arranged her funeral but a pastor felt that he should pray for her and immediately she was healed. Through her healing hundreds were saved. There are now more than twenty-four evangelical churches in Almalonga, bars have closed and the violence has declined. The four jails have closed, and everything is totally different.

The land affected

The unusual dynamic of transformation in Almalonga has been to do with the land. What was once arid soil has now become a fertile valley with as many as three harvests a year. Carrots the length of a man's arm are commonplace, and radishes are harvested within twenty-five days. Before the change took place four trucks of produce would leave the town each month but now trucks leave forty times each week! Christian farmers now drive new Mercedes trucks, and attribute the increase to the Lord.

Trygve and Barbro made the visit to Guatemala with twenty church leaders, and they testify to the validity of the revival. 'What happened there was marvellous,' Trygve told me. He was particularly amazed that in the agricultural changes no mechanical machines or tractors were used and yet the ground was forty times more productive. Trygve invited Mariano, the key leader within Almalonga, for a ten-day visit to Norway. During this time civic dignitaries, representatives of government and the police attended the meetings, and were open to be prayed for.

Prayer has been a vital ingredient in this story. Fifteen thousand people gathered recently in the Market Square to pray and thank God for His kindness.

Story 3 – Betel, Spain (and across the world)

This story is about the incredible transformation of lives from all over the world; it's the story of lives that have been gripped by addictions being set free. A full account of Betel can be found in *We Dance Because We Cannot Fly*, a book by Dr Guy Chevreau.[2] Elliott Tepper is the International Director of Association Betel and it has been my privilege to know Elliott and Mary, his wife, for many years. Following a significant time of ministry in Mexico, they sensed that God was directing them to Spain. The early days in Spain were very difficult, and Elliott began his ministry by preaching on the streets. One of his first converts was Raul Casto, who was to become the first indigenous pastor. I briefly met Raul on my first visit to Spain. He later died of AIDS, but by that time seeds of transformation had been planted into many lives. The church in Madrid is now the largest protestant church in Spain. Three-quarters of the congregation have previously been addicted to heroin. Almost all have been in prison at some time in their lives and eight out of every ten of the younger women in this church have been prostitutes.

Betel is now active in nine nations of the world and forty thousand drug addicts have come through their open doors.

Although I have visited works in Spain my main contact has been with Kent and Mary-Alice Martin who are the UK directors. Having known them for many years I have been greatly blessed by their friendship, and in particular with the Betel family in Birmingham. The Martins left the USA in April 1991 and began their work in Spain, but by 1995 they had found themselves in Birmingham, England. The work began, and Windmill House with a five-acre estate, became available to them through the goodwill of the Cadbury family. Since then other properties have been secured in Nottingham and Derby.

Transformed lives

Betel stands today at the forefront of addiction rehabilitation programmes. Men and women are helped to break free from addictions without dependency on substitutes. This is different from most other programmes and the success rate is higher. The following are some of the highlights of the ministry of Betel:

▶ **The offer of freedom in Christ**

At our Ground Level Leadership conference this year eight of those who are currently on the programme gave testimony, and each one concluded with the words '. . . and I am free!'

▶ **Restoring of dignity and respect**

The change in the young men and women's lives is remarkable. Many of them, as they leave Betel, are totally unrecognisable.

▶ **Work ethic**

The Betel regime is hard. Everyone on the programme has to contribute to his or her upkeep by working – though they are received into the centres free of charge – and small businesses have been set up to support the work. In Birmingham, a second-hand furniture shop operates within the city centre. Furniture is lovingly restored to a high standard and Betel vans collect and distribute it across the area.

▶ **Churches planted**

As men and women break free, churches are planted. Often relatives of those on the programme attend when they see the change that has taken place in their loved ones' lives. The knock-on effect for the community is amazing. At the time of writing, housing benefit funds have been withheld by the 'powers that be' and the base in Birmingham, naturally speaking, struggles for survival. The reality is that government agencies are being saved vast amounts of money as lives are being changed and transformation takes place. However, Betel is predominantly a faith ministry and God is the one who provides.

Notes
1. *Transformations 1* video by Global Net Productions.
2. Guy Chevreau, *We Dance Because We Cannot Fly* (Sovereign World, 2000).

Chapter 14

Transformation – the Territory

When Christianity invades a city

I have lived in the city of Lincoln all my life. Great changes have taken place through the years, but the last ten years have seen amazing movement. The once sleepy rural city with small town atmosphere has, like Gulliver, been stirring itself. With the building of a new university in the city centre the growing student population has been accompanied by new businesses, buildings, restaurants and public houses. For many years Lincoln has been bypassed. The mainline trains miss us by sixteen miles and likewise, the main A1 road to the North and South has, until recently, been connected to the city via an A road that is not designed to carry heavy traffic. At the time of writing this it is currently being developed into a dual carriageway and our city is increasingly being 'placed on the map'. House prices have risen accordingly and the region is fast becoming a desirable place to live. It is my deep desire that these changes should not be confined to its physical well-being but that there should be spiritual growth and development. I love living in Lincoln.

Lincoln has had a chequered spiritual history. One of the first Christian settlements in Britain was in Lincoln. As a city, its history was bright and prosperous. The nine-hundred-year-old Cathedral stands majestically on the top of the hill as a symbol of past spiritual life and achievement. John Wesley found the city friendly, and William Booth also spoke well of it. As a boy, I remember numerous Methodist chapels in our region that spoke of a better past. However, through the years walls have been broken down, and our spiritual heritage undermined. When

103

driving home late at night one of my greatest joys is seeing the
floodlit Cathedral come into view, and I long for the day when
Lincoln will be a light to the world.

Some time ago, whilst reading the gospel of Matthew, I
noticed a number of references to town or city. This led me on
to study about how towns and cities can be impacted by the
gospel. I also began to realise that often the culture of the city
more readily invades the culture of the Church, rather than the
Church invading the city with the culture of the Kingdom.

G. Campbell Morgan, when serving as pastor of Westminster
Chapel in London, saw the importance of this principle. In his
observations on the book of 1 Corinthians, he writes:

> 'What the church supremely needs is to correct the spirit
> of the age. The church in Corinth, catching the spirit of
> Corinth, became anaemic, weak, and failed to deliver the
> message of God to Corinth. The church of God, in London
> invaded by the spirit of London, the materialism, militar-
> ism, sordidness, and selfishness of London, is too weak to
> save London.'[1]

The following seven principles from the gospel of Matthew,
and illustrated in the book of Acts of the Apostles show how
territories can be invaded by the gospel of Christ.

1. Encourage infiltration

'You are the salt of the earth.'   (Matthew 5:13)

The scattering of believers through a city to speak good news and
be good news always makes a difference. People of a different
spirit will halt decay and bring purity and spiritual life.

2. Gain visibility

'You are the light of the world. A city on a hill cannot be hidden.'
(Matthew 5:14)

In Britain today there seems to be a movement away from
'gathered' church. I believe this could prove to be a great mistake.
Though the world, with its post-modern mindset, shies away
from institutions and power-bases, the Church needs to understand that visibility and radiance are things that can show

Kingdom life. The world needs to hear the stories and see that the Church of Jesus is very much alive.

3. Confront darkness

'Then the whole town went out to meet Jesus.'

(Matthew 8:34)

This was in the context of a demon-possessed man being delivered. With this clash of kingdoms the result brought a reaction. In Acts 13:8, a Jewish sorcerer, Elymas, opposed Paul. This clash resulted in salvation. In Acts 16:16, Paul found that Philippi opened up to the gospel when a slave girl with a familiar spirit was released from oppression. As the light shines, darkness disappears and territory is taken.

4. Demonstrate God's power

In Matthew 9:1–8 a paralysed man is healed. Jesus came to His own town and *'when the crowd saw this, they were filled with awe'* (Matthew 9:8). When God's power is released communities are impacted. There are a number of *Transformation* videos available today that tell the stories of whole communities that have turned to Christ through seeing his power displayed. This is again illustrated in Acts 3:1–11 when Peter and John heal a crippled man, and in Acts 28:1–10 when Paul shakes off a deadly snake from his hand without suffering any adverse consequences. It was recorded, *'many who heard the message believed'* (Acts 4:4).

5. Make contacts

'Whatever town or village you enter, search for some worthy person there and stay at his house until you leave.'

(Matthew 10:11)

In Acts 16:13–15 Lydia proved to be this *'worthy person'* and in Acts 18:2–4, Aquilla and Priscilla became keys to the community as Paul *'stayed and worked with them'* (Acts 18:3). If only we could find a person of peace in every village and community who could unlock the territory. God has His ways of making sure that the right person is in the right place at the right time. The key for every believer is the simple truth, 'I can make a difference.'

6. Pursue unity

> *'Every kingdom divided against itself will be ruined, and every city or household divided against itself will not stand.'*
>
> (Matthew 12:25)

For cities to be reached believers must unite. This remains a major challenge as most of us have our own agendas. I recently heard of a conference on 'transformation' where the delegates were encouraged to ask for help. For a great catch of fish all available boats are required. We will never reach our communities on our own. Perhaps we need to say, 'Come over and help us!'

7. Exalt Jesus

> *'When Jesus entered Jerusalem, the whole city was stirred and asked, "Who is this?"'*
>
> (Matthew 21:10)

The triumphal entry of Jesus into Jerusalem caused a stir. The city that Ezra and Nehemiah had rebuilt in their time now became a place where the Messiah placed His feet. Their work, battling and planning had been part of a welcome for this exalting of the King of kings. Ultimately, this is our highest priority; to see Jesus exalted and His Kingdom extended. The part we play matters.

The last thirty years have brought great changes to the Church in Britain. It is now time to see this life spread beyond our walls and structures into the communities where we live. The last chapters for the Church in this nation have yet to be written.

> *'Come, let us rebuild the wall of Jerusalem.'* (Nehemiah 2:17)

Note

1. G. Campbell Morgan, *The Message of the Books of the Bible* (Hodder and Stoughton).

Appendix A

A Simple and Personal Mapping of the New Church movement in Britain

by Stuart Bell

The condition of the Church in Great Britain in late 1960s early 1970s

- Church attendance beginning to decline
- Formalism and tradition
- Growing liberal emphasis
- Dynamic models of evangelism outside existing church circles, e.g. coffee-bar evangelism – Youth for Christ
- The Jesus revolution
- A generation desiring to break out but also looking for roots

Back to the Bible

Many, during this period, began to look into New Testament patterns and structures. The following issues began to come into focus:

- The place of the Scriptures
- The plan of salvation
- The preaching of the Gospel
- The presence of miracles
- The power of the Holy Spirit
- The purpose of the Church

Issues of fellowship, communion and new forms of worship, and the use of homes began to become important.

Help from Church history

During this period of time lessons began to be learned from Church history.

Methodism

The Methodist movement radically impacted the nation. John Wesley structured for discipleship, with small units known as 'class meetings'. He also sought biblical Christianity, with a special emphasis toward the poor, and was known by some as the grandfather of Pentecostalism. His brother, Charles Wesley, captured 'the revival' in the writing of many new hymns.

The Pentecostals

Today's new churches will often point back to the beginning of the 20th century. The century began with an extraordinary visitation of God in a warehouse and horse stable at 312 Azusa Street in Los Angeles.

The Charismatic movement

In the 1960s and 1970s, the experience of the baptism in the Holy Spirit began to move beyond the Pentecostal churches. God broke into an Episcopalian church, again in Los Angeles, where Dennis Bennett was the leader. His experience recorded in *Nine O'clock in the Morning*[1] quickly spread across the world. In England, on 29th September 1964, Michael Harper formed the influential Fountain Trust, which soon published *Renewal* magazine. Other prominent names such as Denis Clark, Arthur Wallis, Campbell McAlpine, Barney Coombs and Roger Forster began to emerge.

The Charismatic movement spread across all boundaries and denominations.

The House Church movement

Many were finding personal renewal – but often came into conflict with existing church structures. It became inevitable that the 'new wine' being poured out needed 'new wineskins'. This often led to people gathering in homes, seeking to rediscover genuine church life. The church was no longer being viewed in terms of buildings but was being seen as people.

An important book, helping many on their journey was *In the Day of Thy Power* by Arthur Wallis.[2]

Restoration

As the new movement grew, the concept of restoration began to capture people's imaginations. Not only were the gifts of the Holy Spirit for today, but also a future church was being seen in terms of revival, a church of splendour. Ephesians 4:11 ministry gifts of apostles, prophets, evangelists, pastors and teachers were no longer seen as confined to the days of the Bible but were given to today's church. Also, a prophetic call towards unity was being proclaimed through *Come Together*, a musical launched in Britain with the help of Jean Darnall. The words, 'You are the people of God and He loves you and has chosen you for His own,' pointed people towards a new kind of church.

Worship

Creative new styles of worship began to emerge. Scriptures began to be sung. Graham Kendrick, Chris Bowater, Noel Richards and many others began to emerge and pipe organs began to feel the challenge.

Bible Weeks

Capel Bible Week was one of the first to carry the genes of the new movement. This was later to be followed by the Dales Bible Week, Stoneleigh, Grapevine and many others. The church was beginning to celebrate again.

Ministry

Ordinary people began to understand that they could contribute and were gifted and valuable.

Emerging teams

The House Church movement was gifted with leaders who wanted to see a different kind of church emerge. This led to some tension in terms of style, approach and doctrinal emphasis. *Restoring the Kingdom* by Dr Andrew Walker[3] tried to identify the differences within the new movement and broadly categorised two groups as R1 and R2, the second being seen as less structured and more grace orientated.

Prior to breakdown in relationships, the early 'fathers' of the movement were amusingly titled 'The Magnificent Seven' consisting of Arthur Wallis, Bryn Jones, David Mansell, Peter Lyne, Graham Perrins, Hugh Thompson and John Noble.

- The 'Fabulous Fourteen' added Gerald Coates, George Tarleton, Barney Coombs, Maurice Smith, Ian McCulloch, John Macloughlan and Campbell McAlpine.

- The fourteen were then to grow to twenty and among those added were Terry Virgo.

- The divisions tended to centre on legalism and freedom. However, as the years passed divisions have been healed and apostolic team leaders have often met together for fellowship.

A team of men including Terry Virgo, Gerald Coates, Derek Brown, Tony Morton, Barney Coombs, Roger Forster, Stuart Bell, Philip Mohabir, David Matthews, Graham Perrins, Peter Lyne, John Noble and David Day met together consistently for a number of years before more numbers were added including Simon Matthews and Paul Reid.

Growth
The House Church movement soon became known as the New Church movement but as the years pass, the movement needs to be ready for the next move of the Spirit.

Notes
1. Dennis Bennett, *Nine O'Clock in the Morning* (Bridge Logos, 1970).
2. Arthur Wallis, *In the Day of Thy Power* (Christian Literature Crusade, 1956).
3. Dr Andrew Walker, *Restoring the Kingdom* (Hodder and Stoughton, 1985).

Appendix B

A Strategy for Church Planting in the Humber to the Wash Region

by Dr Pete Atkins

The need

In the East Midlands, UK, we find ourselves in a situation where church attendance is declining rapidly (6.4% Sunday attendance in 1998); the influence of Christianity on society is waning, and the vast majority of young people particularly, are no longer engaging in church life. We are part of a nation that has the highest teenage pregnancy rate and drug usage rate in Europe, 180,000 abortions annually, high levels of crime on our streets, prisons that are overflowing, and a flood of non-Christian spiritualities invading our contemporary culture. It seems as though our spiritual walls are indeed broken down and breached, our gates burned with fire, and the future compromised and uncertain.

The vision

The vision is to see the trend reversed and to see the Kingdom of God re-established in a major fashion in this region. We want to see the region, in all aspects of its life transformed by the love and power of God in Jesus.

The objective

For some years Ground Level have articulated the objective of seeing 'a cell in every village, a congregation in every town and a celebration in the city from the Humber to the Wash.'[1] This objective encompasses the presence of effective cells etc. of any Christian denomination or stream. Thus, the operational plan is to see a major re-establishment of Christianity in this area, realised in part by starting, where necessary, new Christian communities which serve and engage with the communities in which they are set. This operational plan then is primarily a Church Planting Strategy.

The Strategy

Since December 2000, leaders from the Ground Level Network have been developing a Church Planting Strategy aimed at engaging all constituents of the church in the Humber to Wash area of the East Midlands in a planting process. This geographical area corresponds with the old county boundary of Lincolnshire and is coterminous with the Anglican Diocese of Lincoln and the Lincoln and Grimsby district of the Methodist Church, hence making multi-denominational cooperation much easier administratively.

The Strategy being developed is best described in six tracks which together make an integrated whole. The tracks correspond to some of the key elements of Nehemiah's approach to the rebuilding of Jerusalem's walls:

1. Vision and leadership
2. Prayer
3. Research
4. Equipping
5. Planting (building)
6. Youth and young people (not explicit in Nehemiah but vital in terms of focus for the church currently)

1. Vision and leadership
This involves the leaders of the major Christian groups in the region seeking, developing, owning and presenting God-given vision to reach the region – this could be seen as a regional DAWN vision. Ground Level have taken initiative in this, but we are moving towards a joint approach – led by those with strategic

responsibility for the wider church in the region. Discussions so far have involved the Anglican bishops, the head of the Methodist Church, Assemblies of God and Stuart Bell (leader of Ground Level Network). Catholic, Baptist, Salvationist and other leaders are gradually being engaged. We have developed an advisory team to the initiative, which includes the national experts in church planting from the Methodist, Anglican and Assemblies of God churches as well as an American based mission director attached to our Network.

2. Prayer

We have a dedicated team of people who feel called to pray particularly for this initiative as it develops. This team are updated monthly as to the current issues and meet together for prayer every three months with the Ground Level team member primarily responsible for developing the work. In addition, prayer for the strategy is promoted through local prayer networks such as a 'prayer wall' – a mechanism for ensuring twenty-four hour prayer cover for the region when fully developed, and other prayer teams in the region willing to take this on.

3. Research

We have currently commissioned a researcher (who is a member of one of our local churches) to create a database of all the churches and Christian ministries in the region. Ground Level and Churches Together in All Lincolnshire are jointly funding the work. A multi-denominational team oversees this research and the results will be presented at appropriate intervals to the heads of denominations/new church streams together to aid common strategic planning and guide further prayer and research. The researcher is also studying a cross-denominational cohort of churches in the region that are seen by their denominational heads to be growing and effective. This element of the work is designed to discover what elements are present in growing churches in our geography and culture, which may also be worth noting in caring for and encouraging existing churches as well as for planting new communities of faith. The next phase of the research will be to monitor trends in church presence and strength, identify the gaps in communities or people groups and describe the nature of the 'field' we are working in – demographically, socio-culturally, spiritually, age specific etc.

4. Equipping

We have developed a Church Planting School for the region, which is in its second year (2003). The school seeks to support and encourage any Christian initiative in the region, aimed at reaching a community or people group by starting a new Christian community within it. The school aims to get alongside any kind of new initiative: a second service, a youth congregation, a cell or congregational plant, a parallel plant or other model. The school affirms variety in models of planting and is available for teams from any denomination or stream. The church planting leads nationally for the Anglican, Methodist and Assemblies of God denominations and delivers the teaching and some coaching alongside 'New Church' leaders. The modus operandi includes a teaching, application and case study stream with a parallel coaching (on site) stream.

5. Planting

Currently the Church Planting School is involved with ten planting sites, all of which represent initiatives taken by local churches in the region. It is envisaged, however, that in response to the strategic vision held by the denominational and New Church leaders in the region together, that new initiatives may arise from their overview of the region with resources identified by them from within their respective spheres. Once the current research is producing analysis of Christian deployment in the region and stimulating further prayer, it may well be that the regional church leaders put a proactive planting program in place.

6. Youth and young people

It is felt that a focus on the under thirties is so vital for the present and future church that it deserves a separate 'track' within the overall strategy. This track was the last to be initiated and little joint work has yet been attempted. However, Ground Level is seeking to address the issue amongst its own churches and the past year has seen several initiatives:

- Deliberate engagement with the eighteen to thirty age group in our churches researching relevant issues.
- The beginnings of a church plant into a university in the region.

- The recruitment of a full-time youth work development worker for the network, who will lead this track as part of their work.

- The identification of a substantial amount of money for investment in youth engagement through the Network churches in partnership with this central resource.

- The pilot inclusion of teenagers in the Church Planting School to learn and to be a visible focus for planting teams.

It is worth repeating that the individual tracks of this strategy are part of an integrated whole and each complements and makes possible the effectiveness of the others.

We believe this strategy to be developed in response to the leading and prompting of God with a biblical pattern discerned and founded in the book of Nehemiah. We fully recognise our dependence on God to succeed. We envisage a twenty-year(+) timeframe for its full fruition, and fully acknowledge our constant need for flexibility, a prayerful humble servant attitude, and a desire to maintain the unity of the Spirit across the churches in the region as we work together for the Kingdom of God. We also recognise that this is but one part of the constellation of plans God creates in order to reach all mankind (or just this region) with knowledge of Him. We seek primarily to cooperate with Him and seek to come to a place when our objective is reached and all see that *'this work had been done with the help of our God'* (Nehemiah 6:16).

Note
1. The Humber River and the Wash essentially encompass the northern and southern dimensions respectively of historic Lincolnshire – part of the current East Midlands region of the UK.

Appendix C

Impressions of the Dream Centre, Los Angeles

by Hannah Atkins

I arrived at the airport at twelve o'clock and, as instructed, asked where I could get the Super Shuttle train. The Super Shuttle turned out to be a minibus, which took me all the way to the Dream Centre for $23. The first time I saw it was from the freeway; this huge white building set on a hill with 'THE DREAM CENTRE' emblazoned on the top in big letters. I came to what looked like some form of entrance and found a couple of guys I could ask for directions to the short-term missions office. One guy took me, through a maze of stairways, to the sixth floor of the wrong building! On arriving at the wrong office I phoned for the right office! Anna, the Short-terms Missions Director, came and found me, thankfully bringing with her a guy, Aaron, the Dream Centre assistant, who took my suitcase – thank you, God!

We arrived at an elevator, at which point Anna asked if I wanted to go on one of the homeless missions. The only problem was that they left straight away! Did I trust Aaron to put my bags in my room – 'cause I needed to go! So I left my bags with Aaron and was put in a minibus full of six guys I'd never seen in my life before, ranging from eighteen years old to forty, on my way to 'Skid Row' – the roughest homeless capital of Los Angeles – the homeless capital of the USA! I'm glad my Mum didn't know! James the driver was a character! He told us all so much information; about Azusa Street revival and the house it started from (we were going to visit that after giving out food); the Four Angels Church; the area we were on our way to; Billy's ministry and background.

Billy was driving the van full of the team in front of us. He had been running this mission for eleven years after an amazing encounter with God whilst dealing and doing drugs (including heroine). Along with his wife and two boys, he now feeds thousands of people a week. All the food is donated but he raises money to support the mission and his family through T-shirts and a CD of his own guitar music.

Skid Row

We arrived at Skid Row – an area about five blocks by four blocks and lined with tents and cardboard boxes, housing thousands of homeless drug addicts, alcoholics and prostitutes – people of all ages, kids, men and women, young and old. It looked unbelievable, and the people looked desperate – their bodies and minds desperate for their next shoot up, but their hearts desperate for life. Everyone just lived in fear. I met a guy called Danny in the food line – he was cool and I wanted to chat to him. It took a few minutes to get him even to look in my direction, but five minutes later he was telling me his story, making full eye contact within ten minutes. He had lived here for eighteen months after starting his addiction to cocaine. Before then, he was happily living with his fiancée in a house on the other side of town. He turned to drugs after his fiancée and baby died during childbirth. One of the mother's heart valves had burst and they were unable to save either her or the baby. He was heart-broken and all he could think of to sooth his anger was to shoot up. He'd been there ever since, addicted to coke and was still kicking cold turkey off heroine. I talked to him for a while – about Billy's ministry etc. He said he wasn't into the whole 'full-on' God stuff, but that he was a firm believer. He was sick of this life but couldn't leave without being followed – if he was caught leaving the area, there was a contract killer on his case. He owed money for drugs and his earnings had been stolen.

'If we get what we want, others suffer without what they need.'

I headed back up to Anna's office and she showed me my room. It was a dormitory for eight people that I had to myself. Each dorm had four bunk beds and a toilet and sink in a room attached. Everything in the whole building was whitewashed and clean, but really basic. In fact, that was one of the first impressions I got on arrival at the Dream Centre. The complex is huge but everything looked quite old. Clean, but far from glamorous. In all honesty, I was a little disappointed at first, but later Anna told me the amount of money that was spent on food and missions everyday. This money could have been spent on the building – but they cared more about the poor. Wow!

Youth Fuego

We rounded up about twenty kids and all piled in a bus to go to the Centre. On arrival, we made our way up to the gym where 'Youth Fuego' (*fuego* being Spanish for 'fire') was held. It is a big gym and looked impressive with ping-pong tables, a tuck shop, a great stage with two big video screens, a corner with a few guys break dancing and a table football. The atmosphere was great. The kids loved it. I sat at the back for a few minutes, just watching people, to take it all in. Though I felt very anti-social, I wandered around and chatted to different youth, watched the breakers etc.

I found a spot near the breakers and took a seat next to some of the kids I had been sitting with on the bus. The meeting began with worship, led by a really great band. The music really struck me. Worship leader 'Heather' caught my eye. She led really well – stunning with an amazing voice and really able to get the kids going. The music was really rocky guitar stuff and the kids really got into it.

This was followed by some games, led by a really young trendy girl, who I later found out was the youth pastor for the whole thing. I think one of the most amazing things about the Dream Centre for me, was seeing all these girls of my own age in action. Their hearts were so hungry for God, so loving for the kids, so sold out for the vision, so brilliant at leading and so admirable! I learnt so much from them.

Michelle, the youth pastor, gave a really inspiring few words, followed by a series of three testimonies from the kids. They were really moving. God really does change people's lives around! This was followed by a bit more worship, this time led by Michelle. She is such a motivator and no one messes!

After the meeting, I went to the Master's Commission (discipleship training) floor and hung out with them all till I was ready to drop. I slept so well!

Wake-up call

Up at 6.15am, I called for Anna at 7.00am and we went for breakfast. After breakfast we went to a prayer meeting at the same gym. There were at least fifty people in there wandering around praying, reading the Bible or writing. The God-atmosphere was incredible again. After spending some time praying in the corner, I just cried for about an hour! God broke my heart. I was so humbled. I just came back to the realisation of the grace on my life, and my inadequacy without Jesus. As I felt like I was being held in God's arms, I had images of girls being abused in the arms of their pimps or clients. That really broke me. I just kept thinking 'Lord – please use me in whatever way You want. I'm so desperate to serve You.' I got to the point where I thought I could give up my whole life and stay there. But I knew that I just had to be there at that point, and then God would remind me of His heart for me in Manchester.

At this heart-broken point of mascara all over my face and snot in undesired places, to my horror the lights were turned on. To my horror again, the door that I was sitting beside was the main exit – great! My humbling day!

I went back with Anna and had some time in my room to collect my thoughts before the team meeting at 8.45am.

The grand tour!

We met in the conference room, this time with Abi (the most lovely Australian girl), Greg and his nephew John (from Ohio) and Anna. Anna left us watching the Dream Centre video, which was great. She then took us on a tour around the Centre. On the rooftop she told us of the amazing story behind the building . . .

Matthew Barnett had come over about nine years ago to pastor a church in Los Angeles. He had about thirty old people in his congregation. One week he decided to move the piano from one side of the church hall to the other, at which point half the congregation left! By the end of six months, he had a hand-ful of people left. Even the team he had taken with him left discouraged.

One day he had an amazing dream, of having a multi-ministry centre for the poor. He decided that they needed a building. At the same time, the Four Angels Hospital was up for sale. It was a multi-complex hospital building but they wanted $25 million for it! No one had shown any interest for months. The only people who used it were the film industry – different films had been shot there, like *Apollo 13* and *Tomb Raider*.

Matthew Barnett really felt that they should have this building and offered them $3 million. They accepted $5, but wanted a non-returnable deposit of $500,000 straight away and the rest paid off within eighteen months. With a handful of people in his congregation, most of them homeless, God provided the whole amount to the very last dollar, the day before it was due. Wow! Most of it came from individual donations, from all kinds of people and places. It's an amazing story! From that point the building was completely theirs, debt free! Since then they have seen numerous miracles of money coming in, to renovate the whole place.

The food van

We met out on the 'black top' – the Dream Centre car park – after lunch. We went straight to work; packing fruit and yoghurt in plastic bags ready to feed about three hundred families at two different locations in the area. My job was to pack fifteen bananas in a bag and pass it on to the next lady in the production line. There were six of us working in the food lorry, three Philippinos, two Americans, two Australians (Abi, and one named Claire who ran this ministry), and me!

The first stop was only a few minutes away, at the Dream Centre's church. Already there was a queue of about forty people, some of them mothers with children.

I travelled with the American guys in their hired car, following the lorry. As we crossed the road to meet them, I was allocated to the job of giving the bags out. I think this was the best job! I got to smile and talk with the women, whilst handing them a bag of really nice food. This time, the government provided the food and this ministry packed and delivered it. Everyone who received a bag had to sign and write down his or her address.

I chatted to Claire for a while. She's the loveliest girl. Her Dad organises the Hillsong Conference in Australia! I thought that was cool! She had come to the Dream Centre eighteen months ago, for the same reason as I had! She was only planning to stay a while, to grasp the heart for the Centre, then go and set one up back at home. God had different plans!

She sounded really interested in what we want to do in Manchester. I invited her over. She's been to England a few times and really loves it. I hope she comes.

I invited so many people over the last day! Well, if God wants them to come and help us, then I'd love it!

Hope for Homeless Youths

Abi and I went for tea. We sat with Rowan (missions director) and Aaron (director assistant – I think!). It was so cool because everyone on the leadership team is in their early or mid twenties. They really inspired me – and made me laugh! After tea, I met another team outside the Hope for Homeless Youth House. This was another really great ministry. The lady in charge gave us the run-down of the vision, values and practicalities of the ministry we were about to be involved with.

I went back in the van with the team and this mentalist driver! We did the whole 'singing thing' and they made me sing a song to them. This other girl sang too – it was all very fun/funny!

Very tired, I pretty much went straight to bed!

BADD

I had breakfast with Abi, and then decided to go to the BADD Bible study. BADD stands for 'born again and delivered disciples'. It is a programme that takes on girls and guys from about 16+ that have come out of prison and are on parole etc. Sometimes the jury gives them an option as to whether they want to stay in prison or go on the BADD programme. It's hard-core! Quite scary, seeing single file lines of people walking through the Dream Centre shouting, 'Yes sir,' etc.! I went to the Bible study on my own and was quite intimidated walking into a room of about two hundred people, all facing my way!

It was more like a service – we sang some worship songs and then a lady got up to speak. She sounded well hard! She talked about when she'd overdosed, at a really low point in her life but how God had other plans for her life and how she was now leading the BADD programme! Then, her husband got up to speak! He was so funny! He shouted everything – all great stuff about being over-comers. He admitted that he was 'trying to scare the Hell out of us!' These BADD guys had been up since 5.30 am and it was now about 8 am. One of the girls on the programme had her eyes shut. Unfortunately for her, he saw her ... **'Get those eyes open now** ... listen to me – these words are not mine – they bring life – **this is life. Sit up and listen!'**

Ah! He was scary, but I had so much respect for him. He was so real about life and what matters. He'd been through it all and had an amazing encounter with God when he was in his twenties. He'd overdosed so much that he was paralysed in his bed for four days and thought he was going to die. He had cried out to God and said, 'If You exist then get me out of here and I will live the rest of my life for You.' That's exactly what he's done!

Metro-Kidz

Next we went down to the 'Metro-Kidz' office, where we packed and labelled T-shirts. It's not always fun working there! We finished early and I went to buy the Dream Centre's video and CD, then head up to Anna's office.The plan was to go to Hollywood and then come back to pack, pay and clean before going to the airport.

We were so pushed for time. A message had been left for me in Anna's office saying that I had to get an earlier flight and needed to be at the airport really soon. Several phone-calls later, Anna had arranged a lift for me, and I had to be back at the Centre, packed and ready to go in about an hour and a half.

Mardy bum!

I had to wait a bit at the airport, so I started to write up more of this account. When boarding the plane, I was adamant that I wasn't going to talk to anyone but just get on with my writing. The plane was only half full and I spotted a whole row free at the back. Loads of space and loads of turbulence – ace! There was a guy about my age sitting in the row behind me. I deliberately didn't make eye contact and hoped he wouldn't think I had sat there to talk to him! I sat by the window and got my book out – trying to be as anti-social as possible. Then I heard, 'So what have you been doing here in Los Angeles?' I answered with as few un-provocative words as I could think of, but he kept asking questions. I was giving one word 'I really don't want to talk to you' answers when he mentioned that he was reading his Bible! This caught my attention a little more and I turned round and asked if he was a Christian. He said, 'Yes,' and asked me the same. It turned out that he had been praying for a Christian to sit where I had sat! He'd never met a Christian on the plane before! We chatted for a bit more and to cut a long story short. He was called Ben and played football (soccer I think!) for Virginia! He asked more questions about what I did etc., and after telling him all about the massive vision, he said that he wanted to support it as his charity! He had also been praying about what to give money to, and he felt that this was the right thing! Ace – thanks God and sorry for being so mardy at the beginning of the flight!

So all in all it was so good! I learnt loads and have been inspired to dream bigger still!

Appendix D

Partnership without Ownership – a Tale of Three Networks

by Stuart Bell

In transformation stories that I have heard of in cities and communities around the world, it has become obvious to me that new ways to go forward have been found. Prayer has certainly played a major part, but also there has been a need to break with mediocrity. There have been high levels of humility demonstrated by those who have pursued unity and though vision has been strong, there seems to have been a strange absence of hidden agendas. One thing essential for 'transformation' is the need to deal with the issue of 'control'. Running through the veins of most visionary leaders is a desire to succeed. With the best intentions in the world, there can still be a mixture of motives. In my own limited experience, I have recognised an inner tendency to want to put my 'stamp' on things and there is so often the hidden need for recognition and affirmation. So often we can say the right words, but I have learned that what goes on in the human heart can be tainted.

In the last few years I have been deeply challenged by what I would call 'partnership without ownership'. I have, for most of my Christian life, recognised the need for unity and have understood the fact that two is better than one. However, it is only recently that I have discovered the principle from Philippians of looking, not only to my own interests, but also that of the interests of others. In fact, Scripture challenges and encourages us to consider others better than ourselves. It has been my joy to see some of these principles worked out in cooperation with teams in other nations. Our desire is to partner together for the sake of the Kingdom, without having to have our particular flag planted in someone else's territory. The following stories fill me with a great sense of gratitude to God, who seems to have orchestrated things to enable this bigger and healthier picture to emerge. I will endeavour to explain:

More than twenty years ago I planted a small fellowship in the north area of the city of Lincoln. I found myself leading a group of mostly un-churched young people who wanted to know more about being followers of Jesus. During this time, knowing it was not good to be isolated or independent, I wrote to a number of churches in our region to enquire if there was a desire among the leaders to meet together for prayer, fellowship and to share with one another. To my surprise, a number of them began to gather together and, because we offered no threat to them, we became a kind of catalyst, giving leaders space to be together without fear of being 'taken over'. Following the usual 'honeymoon' period it became clear to us that some of these relationships had a sense of divine connection. Not knowing what to do, I sought the advice of Gerald Coates, who helped me clarify vision and put together a team of key leaders who had a desire to see the gospel being more clearly proclaimed within our region. This group soon became known as the 'Ground Level' team, and before long we began an exciting journey together, which has involved planting churches, serving churches, and the birth and overseeing of our annual Bible week, 'Grapevine', which attracts thousands each year to our local area. More churches have been added to our network and regular leadership forums meet throughout the year. For many years church life has been quite static. Working with Ground Level has produced for us a more dynamic model, where ministries can be more flexible and be released to serve the wider Body of Christ. As we have learned from teams that have more experience than ourselves, there is no doubt that we have experienced the 'favour' of God, which we know we don't deserve.

The East Coast of USA

The second strand of my story again goes back twenty years to the kitchen in the home of Jack Groblewski (Grubby), pastor of New Covenant Christian Community in Bethlehem, Pennsylvania, USA. I passed through his fellowship on a visit organised for me by an evangelist called Eddie Smith, who had been pushing me for some time to go over to the States. Little did I know that when Eddie put together my itinerary it was with some reluctance that Jack invited me to his church. Over coffee in his kitchen a strange thing happened. Jack opened up a map on the table, of the east coast of America and began to tell me of how, on a number of occasions, he had travelled to certain places and prayed that revival would touch these communities. The places where Jack had prayed were 'circled' on the map. To our utter surprise, those ringed towns were the very places I had just visited on my itinerary. These were not well known large cities but relatively small towns in different States on the east coast. As we looked across the table a remarkable thing happened. Our hearts were strangely joined together and from then until today we have been the closest of friends. For many years we have sensed we would one day work more closely together and though there have been many geographic exchanges and family holidays together, it is only quite recently that we have begun to walk into a sense of joined destiny, in ways we would never have imagined years before.

The story continues with an evening at Waverley Abbey House in Surrey, with Dale Gentry, a prophet from Oklahoma. Many received personal words of prophecy and before the close of the meeting Dale shared an unusual 'word' with me. He said, 'I see a bridge between the East Coast of England and the East Coast of America, a bridge that you will often cross.' He also spoke of some kind of leadership on both sides of the bridge and pointed out that, in past history, this bridge had been crossed for the sake of revival On my return, we discovered more fully how connections had been made by the Pilgrim Fathers and in the ministry of John Wesley. Our area has many sites of interest from these two periods in history and a bridge between England and America had been established. A few days later my friends, Pete and Kath Atkins, visited a small bookshop in Stamford, Lincolnshire, and found on the shelves a book written by the Dean of Lincoln Cathedral in 1952 called, *Lincolnshire's Links with the USA*. One morning I was mulling over what these things might mean, when the telephone rang and I was invited to take part in a leaders' conference in the USA. I have to confess I did not even pray about this invitation, I simply sensed God was taking us on an exciting journey. The conference was held in a hotel in Virginia Beach, just a mile from the spot where John Smith,

from Lincolnshire, had landed. It was this man who had
established Virginia. As the conference proceeded I felt more
was happening than I knew about. At the end of the conference
Dick Blackwell, a leader of the team known as Grace Presbytery,
announced that he would like all those leaders to attend Ground
Level's annual conference in England. The following year
twenty-eight of their key leaders honoured us with their
presence in the Hayes Conference Centre in Swanwick, Derbyshire. It was not long before we sensed our paths had crossed in
God's plan, and we agreed a partnership commitment between
Ground Level and the Grace Network of USA. I am thankful we
did not try to 'put our flag' in their soil. We now share a mutual
sense of leadership on both sides of the bridge.

South Africa

The third strand of this story, from my perspective, is no less
exciting.

Some years ago, one of our team members visited South Africa
to learn something about the principles of cell church. During
his visit he left a flyer advertising our forthcoming leaders'
conference in Swanwick, Derbyshire. Unbeknown to us, a group
of apostolic leaders had been sensing that God wanted them to
make contacts within the UK. They were in a process of seeing if
they could visit some of the better-known teams within our
country. On seeing the flyer, a group of South African leaders
decided to visit certain key leaders in the UK and to also tag on a
visit to the Conference in Swanwick. In 1997, a significant group
arrived at our Ground Level Conference knowing nothing of our
work. It was not until the final day that we gave opportunity to
hear from our guests. With some embarrassment we heard them
talk of the many churches they were collectively involved in.
Following this session Irene and I introduced ourselves to
Francois and Ansa Van Niekerk. As we talked together we were
amazed at the similarities of our journey. Within a few months
we were invited to Hatfield Christian Fellowship, a large strategic
church in Pretoria, South Africa, and we found God joining our
hearts. This friendship developed so quickly that it feels as
though we have known one another for years. I am deeply
grateful to God for the help, support and love our church, and
our network, have received from Francois.

One very special afternoon in Lincoln we sat with friends from the USA and South Africa, praying that this threefold chord would not be broken. On that day we were also conscious that others, in due course, would join us as we are determined that our relationships do not become exclusive. We are beginning to benefit enormously from 'Partnership without Ownership' and believe that we will achieve far more by being together, than just doing our own thing. Our prayer is for 'transformation' stories across the world.

If you have enjoyed this book and would like to help us to send a copy of it and many other titles to needy pastors in the **Third World**, please write for further information or send your gift to:

**Sovereign World Trust
PO Box 777, Tonbridge
Kent TN11 0ZS
United Kingdom**

or to the **'Sovereign World'** distributor in your country.

Visit our website at **www.sovereign-world.org**
for a full range of Sovereign World books.